Where Do I Start?

of related interest

Autistic Logistics, Second Edition
A Parent's Guide to Tackling Bedtime, Toilet Training,
Meltdowns, Hitting, and Other Everyday Challenges
Kate Wilde
ISBN 978 1 78775 749 3
eISBN 978 1 78775 750 9

Parenting Rewired
How to Raise a Happy Autistic Child in a Very Neurotypical World
Danielle Punter and Charlotte Chaney
ISBN 978 1 83997 072 6
eISBN 978 1 83997 073 3

Fifteen Things They Forgot to Tell You About Autism
The Stuff That Transformed My Life as an Autism Parent
Debby Elley
ISBN 978 1 78592 438 5
eISBN 978 1 78450 810 4

What Your Autistic Child Wants You to Know
And How You Can Help Them
Maja Toudal
Illustrated by Signe Sønderhousen
Foreword by Tony Attwood
ISBN 978 1 78775 772 1
eISBN 978 1 78775 773 8

Sensory Parenting for Sensory Children
Tanya Van Dalen
ISBN 978 1 83997 254 6
eISBN 978 1 83997 255 3

Where Do I Start?

How to Navigate the Emotional Journey of Autism Parenting

KATE LAINE-TONER

Jessica Kingsley Publishers
London and Philadelphia

First published in Great Britain in 2024 by Jessica Kingsley Publishers
An imprint of John Murray Press

1

Front cover image source: Shutterstock®.

A CIP catalogue record for this title is available from the
British Library and the Library of Congress

ISBN 978 1 83997 552 3
eISBN 978 1 83997 553 0

Printed and bound in Great Britain by TJ Books Limited

Jessica Kingsley Publishers' policy is to use papers that are natural,
renewable and recyclable products and made from wood grown in sus-
tainable forests. The logging and manufacturing processes are expected to
conform to the environmental regulations of the country of origin.

Jessica Kingsley Publishers
Carmelite House
50 Victoria Embankment
London EC4Y 0DZ

www.jkp.com

John Murray Press
Part of Hodder & Stoughton Limited
An Hachette UK Company

Contents

Acknowledgements

I am grateful to many people for making this book happen. First, a huge thanks to Lynda Cooper and Jessica Kingsley Publishers for deciding to publish this book. I am grateful for the opportunity to share so much information with people who truly need it.

Thank you to my eternal cheerleaders, Christina, Cat and Mika. Your encouragement and faith in me means more than words can say. Thank you to Ben for giving me time and space to write. Thank you to Greg for your eternal support. Huge thanks to Jade, Lizzie and Loren, who taught me so much over the years. I'd especially like to thank all the Bristol Autism Support parents and carers who shared their stories, worries and solutions with me. You will always be in my heart.

Huge thanks to you, lovely reader, for picking up this book. I know that it will help you and it makes me happy to know this.

We cannot force someone to hear a message they are not ready to receive, but we must never underestimate the power of planting a seed.

(Unknown)

Preface

Parents of autistic children don't come into the world of autism as enlightened beings. Most begin the journey in fear. While society's awareness and understanding of autism are improving, the media still regularly promotes the message that autism is terrible and scary and something to avoid at all costs. Parents new to autism don't know this isn't true.

This book is intended as a gentle guide for those who are new to autism. It is designed to be read cover to cover, from start to finish. The first and most extensive section is about how a parent can help themselves because, before you can help anyone else, you must get yourself into the right place, mentally and emotionally.

Throughout this book, I share tips and strategies you may be able to use to help your child, yourself and your family. Not everything is going to be right for you. At home, I have a toolbox, and in it are tools I use often, some I use rarely and some I never use. You probably also have a toolbox, but the tools you use more or less often will be different to mine. It is the same with advice about parenting your autistic child.

As I am in the UK, I have included an amount of UK-based information, which I know to be vital to parents and carers living here. However, this book is intended to be a universal guide to managing the emotional aspect of parenting an autistic child. Most of the information will apply to you wherever you are.

Once you have the information you need, you can make a plan of action and move forward in a way that works for you, your child and your family. Without taking on the guidance from the first section of this book, you may remain in a place of fear for far longer than is necessary. Fear is a powerful motivator, but it won't help your child.

I wrote a lot of this book on my phone during a period when my daughter wouldn't let me sit at my computer. I wrote some of it in the wee small hours while she was in bed. I wrote the bulk of it on very little sleep. I am a single mother of an autistic child with Attention Deficit Hyperactivity Disorder (ADHD) and severe learning disability. I have very little support, and my life is often challenging. I tell you this not as a martyr but so that you understand that when I talk about the magic of autism and say that 'autism isn't scary', I'm writing from a place of hard-won experience.

For ease, I use the term 'parents' throughout this book to encompass all those looking after and raising autistic children. I know that you may not be a parent, but a grandparent, an auntie or a foster carer. You are a parent in my eyes.

Where I started

My daughter Emily was around 15 months old when I began to realize that she might be autistic. Developmentally she was significantly delayed. She wasn't walking, and she wasn't talking, and we were quickly moving past that reassuring 'all children develop at different rates' stage.

We took her to a family party with about 30 adults. She sat on the floor for most of the party, oblivious to everyone. It was as though she was alone in the room. I still have a mental picture of her sitting in her little blue jumper, in her own world that none of us felt a part of.

At the time, I'd just relocated to a small village. I had no friends locally (and not many anywhere else either) and was alone all day with my thoughts. Like most parents in this phase of their autism journey, I didn't know anything about the condition other than what the media had fed me about it being something to fear. I spent my days in a panic, throwing money at the situation for lack of knowing what else to do. I bought books that were too scary to read, sensory toys because the internet told me to, and supplements my daughter didn't need.

I have never felt as isolated, frightened and lonely as I did that first year in Autismland.

In 2012 we moved to Bristol. My daughter was diagnosed with autism shortly after we moved (a fast-track assessment pilot was running at the time, and we somehow managed to get a referral). I looked for local support but couldn't find what I was after.

In children's centres, I saw leaflets that advertised support groups for parents of children with additional needs. This would have been helpful, but they were often out of date and had no contact details to find out if they were still happening.

I'd meet people who said things like, 'My sister told me about this great place for autistic children, but I don't remember where it is or what it is called'. I'd smile and say, 'Oh, thanks'. These people mean well, but this kind of pointless information is frustrating at best.

At the time, my daughter was seeing an orthotist. The orthotics clinic sent a map with their appointment letter. The map was of the sort that had been photocopied over and over, to the extent that the street names were illegible. It had a black arrow in the middle pointing to nowhere alongside text that said, 'our building is here'. How helpful.

I wished that there was a place I could go to ask things like, 'Is this group still running?' or 'What's it like at that soft play?' I decided to create a forum that would bring people together to ask these kinds of questions and to share experiences and ideas, joys and fears.

I set up a pub meetup group. At first, there were two of us, then four, then ten. We outgrew the pub and moved to a church hall. We outgrew the church hall and moved to a bigger venue. I organized more meetings, play sessions, pamper days, therapeutic comedy shows, courses and family activities. I set up a Facebook group that, at the time of writing, has over 3300 local members. What started as a tiny idea is now a big, busy charity that supports around 3600 parents and carers at any given time.

As many parents of autistic children do, through my daughter's journey, I realized that I am also autistic and have ADHD. Understanding that I am a neurodivergent adult was a painful realization; I could see how not knowing this about myself had impacted my life (and the lives of the people around me) in a negative way. However, once the dust settled, for the first time in my life, I fit somewhere: I found my tribe with other neurodivergent people and other parents of neurodivergent children.

Over the past 11 years, I've spoken to thousands of parents and carers. I have learned something new from every single one of them. In this book, I aim to distil the wisdom of all those people, alongside my own experience as a parent, a parent supporter and a neurodivergent person.

This is a book about acceptance – acceptance of your child's autism, acceptance of the new life you will need to carve out and possibly acceptance of your own neurodivergence.

There may be things in this book that you are not ready for, and that's OK. Any ideas you are not prepared to manage will be sown as seeds for when your emotional soil is ready to support them.

Parenthood will break you. Raising an autistic child will break you into more, smaller pieces. However, you will find a way to take the pieces and create a new, improved version of yourself. Autism will make you a better parent, a better human being, and a more compassionate citizen of the world.

Autism demands radical acceptance. You must come to accept that your child has a lifelong, neurological condition. For many people, this is a very painful process. You will need to accept the things in your child that are very different from non-autistic children. You will also need to come to terms with how the people around you – friends, relatives and strangers – react and respond to your child.

Raising an autistic child will force you to accept that the world is a harsh place for those who do not fit into society's norms. However, you will meet many people along the way who will restore your faith in humanity.

I never want anyone to feel as isolated and lonely as I felt at the beginning of my journey. May this book be your roadmap to a new world and a new normal. I hope my words will wrap round you like a comforting blanket and give you confidence, courage and hope.

PART 1

How to Help Yourself

I know it will be tempting to skip this part and dive into the advice about helping your child. However, remember what they say about how when you are on a plane that encounters difficulty, you put on your oxygen mask first before helping anyone else. This first section of this book (helping yourself) is the oxygen mask you need before you get to the second section (helping your child).

This is not selfish. If you are in the right headspace, you will be far more able to help your child. Happy, confident parents make happy, confident children.

CHAPTER 1

Autism Isn't Scary

Human beings are hard-wired to spot differences in their surroundings. This ability was incredibly useful and, at times, even life-saving for cave-dwelling hunter-gatherers. Being able to 'spot the difference' helped our ancestors track prey to hunt and feed their families. It enabled them to understand which plants and berries could be eaten and which were poisonous. It also enabled them to interpret the changing seasons and stay cool in the summer and warm and safe in the winter.

We still use these skills today, but our hypersensitivity to differences in our surroundings also has a negative edge. If you saw a flock of blackbirds fly past your window and noticed that among them was one red bird, you would most likely think that this was interesting and beautiful. You might tell a friend or your partner, 'Earlier, I saw this one red bird in a flock of black ones; it was amazing!'

But think of how some people speak about the colleague who never wants to go out for after work drinks or who dresses differently to others. Or the woman in the grocery store queue who is moving sooooo slowly. Or the man with a vocal tic who is shouting in the park. Would most people say, 'That's so interesting and delightful!'? Probably not.

It's important to acknowledge that, before we acclimatize to the world of difference that having an autistic child gives us access to, our own thoughts and words about human variation might have this unkind edge. Before I had a child who makes lots of loud, random noises in public, if I had seen a child like her while out and about, it would have made me uneasy. I would have thought that child was upset or in pain. My ignorance would have made me uncomfortable.

Now I know that those sounds are (generally) contented ones, and the individual making them is simply commenting on their internal landscape and the world around them in a way that feels good to them. Now I smile at the noisy child and the person caring for them. I'm embarrassed to say that in the past, I might have moved away from them instead.

We fear what we don't understand

As I've mentioned, like most parents of autistic children, I knew very little about autism when it first turned up in my life. I only knew what society had fed me: autism is aggressive, isolating and sad. Like most parents, I turned to the internet for help and information. This only reinforced my belief that autism was horrible and that I had to do all I could to eliminate or at least reduce its hold on my child.

Further driving my fear was that, by this point, my daughter had gone from a happy, smiling baby to a distant, insular toddler. She didn't want to be held. She didn't acknowledge me when I walked into a room she was in. Not knowing any better, I thought that this must be our new normal and that she would always be this way.

Fortunately for our family, it was at this point that we moved from a small, remote village to a large city. I began to connect with other parents of autistic children. I started to learn how to find support for my daughter, access help with education and enjoy activities that were available for children with additional needs.

My fear, which had kept me frozen and paralysed, began to ease, and I could move forward in helping my daughter in tangible, practical ways. Over time, I was able to see that it's not autism that is scary. What is scary is professionals' lack of knowledge and understanding of autism. The lack of support available for our children (and for us as carers) is also frightening. Autism in itself is just a condition – like any other – that requires a parent to educate themselves in order to best support their child.

Why do you feel this way?

If you have negative feelings about autism, where did those feelings come from? I grew up in a family that had no understanding of autism or other neurological conditions. People and things that were different to what society labelled as 'normal' were to be feared and avoided. This is no one's fault; it was simply the result of a lack of awareness and comprehension of such things.

Many of us grew up in a time when the word 'retarded' was freely used to describe individuals with learning difficulties or neurological differences. They didn't know what they didn't know. We must also remember that we now have the internet that – sometimes for better and sometimes for worse – helps us to sift through, decipher and assimilate the information we need as parents of children on a different developmental pathway to most. Our parents and others of their generation would have had to visit a library or mail order specialist books to access even a fraction of the information we can find in seconds.

While the ability to recognize differences is hard-wired, for many of us, it was further ingrained by our upbringing. How the people around us responded to and spoke about differences in others and disability can significantly impact how we view the world.

This can create a highly complex set of feelings when we first find ourselves in the world of autism. These kinds of feelings are very typical:

- This can't be autism.

- I am not having this.

- What will my parents/friends/spouse/partner/siblings say?

- This will cause a huge problem (in my family/with my friendship circle).

- I can't manage this.

- I can't cope with this.

- I love my child, but I don't want them to be autistic.

- I must fix this.

- How do I fix this?

- (Cue frantic internet searching and potentially spending a fair amount of money on books, supplements, Epsom salts, and other things you read may 'reduce the symptoms of autism'.)

This is one of those times when we have to do what I call putting the stick in the bicycle wheel. That emotional wheel is spinning, spinning, spinning in your mind, causing so much fear and anxiety. We have to find a way to get a stick into those spokes and stop that wheel from spinning as early on as possible. Only then will you be able to take in the valuable and crucial information that you need to help your child.

If you are frightened by the idea of your child being autistic, why is that? What is that fear based on? The only way out of the fear is to face it head-on. Looking at the emotions I mentioned earlier, we can see that they fall into three different categories:

- 'I believe autism is scary and bad'.

  - This can't be autism.

  - I am not having this on my watch.

  - I love my child, but I don't want them to be autistic.

  - I must fix this.

  - How do I fix this?

- 'I am afraid that the people around me will abandon me if my child is autistic'.

  - What will my parents/friends/spouse/partner/siblings say?

  - This will cause a huge problem (in my family/with my friendship circle).

- 'I won't be able to deal with this successfully'.
    - I can't manage this.
    - I can't cope with this.

Let's unpick these.

'I believe autism is scary and bad'

This is a normal feeling when you don't know anything about autism. We fear what we don't know. If you were to walk into an unknown, unlit building at night, you'd be nervous about who or what was inside. However, once you found the light switch and turned on the lights, you'd see it was just a building. Autism is just the same. Once we know how to find, access and use the help, benefits and strategies available to us, it's no longer scary.

It's also vital for you to understand that the media constantly drip feeds us the erroneous and damaging message that autism is bad and something to be feared. It will take time for you to understand that this is not true, and to see that this is sensationalism designed solely to sell newspapers.

When a parent first begins to think about their child being on the autism spectrum, the urge to somehow fix the situation is intense. You may not know much, if anything, about autism. As caretakers of our children, we have a fierce drive to protect them, and when we don't know better, we can perceive autism as a threat to be eradicated.

Most people do what I did: they buy books and supplements, try special diets, read blogs of parents who 'triumphed over autism', and so on. This is very natural. As parents, we are compelled to keep our children safe from harm, and if we see autism as a bad thing, we want to get shot of it as quickly as possible.

Let's face it, raising children is scary all by itself. A parent's life is full of unknowns, little and big upsets, fears and worries. Autism adds a new set of tasks and things to learn, new layers of worry or perhaps a different vantage point to worry from. Realistically, however, parenting an autistic child is not scarier than parenting any other child. It's just different.

'I'm afraid that the people around me will abandon me if my child is autistic'

I don't know where you are on your journey, and you may have already been through this painful, bramble-filled section. I'm sorry to say that worrying about people close to you abandoning you is a valid concern. Sadly, it is the rare person who comes through this phase of their life with the same support network they went in with.

I'll cover this in detail later on, but for now, I will tell you that when you have to explain to the people around you that you have sought out and received a diagnosis of autism for your child, those people may respond in some very unexpected ways. The people you believed would be most supportive may be the least helpful, and those you thought would turn their back on you may be the most receptive.

There is no predicting how the people in your life will respond, and the loss of friends and family due to their lack of support can be excruciating. In time, however, you will find your tribe among other parents of autistic children. I will tell you how to do this in this book.

'I won't be able to deal with this successfully'

Chances are, if you had to build a birdhouse, bake a cake, or set up a new television, you would not know how to do these things. You would need supplies, ingredients and instructions – whatever would make that project successful. Similarly, if you start a new job or want to learn a new language or skill, at first, you will be a bit wobbly, but in time and with help, you will get there.

You don't even have a map when you first start your autism journey. No one knows how to be a parent to your autistic child. There is no guidebook. But with time, perseverance and making connections with people already in the autism world, you will find the tools to do – at worst – a good job of it.

Many millions of parents before you thought, 'I can't do this', but they did, and you can, too. You will find your way. Autism isn't scary; not knowing what to do to help your child is. Stick with me, and I'll teach you the information you need to know and where to find it.

AUTISM ISN'T SAD

At a recent event, I introduced myself and talked about my work with a woman at my table. She told me about her (peripheral) involvement with a childcare centre that supported autistic children. 'It's so sad', she said, just as the event's presenter began speaking.

I stewed about what the woman had said throughout the morning's proceedings. When we had a break, I explained to her that autism isn't sad. Many things around autism are sad, such as the lack of support, scarcity of school places for autistic children and society's misunderstanding and judgement around the condition.

To say that autism is sad is to say that our children are sad and that I (as an autistic person) am sad, as autism is an integral part of who we are. I pointed out that our autistic children are beautiful and bring so much joy and colour to the world's table. There's nothing sad in that. She thanked me and said what I'd told her was very important and that she would hang onto it and share it with others.

Sometimes we have to educate the world about autism. This is frustrating and, at times, annoying, but if we are all doing it, the world will be a better place.

CHAPTER 2

All the Feels

The parental gut feeling is a highly accurate tool. It is like a finely tuned compass, leading the way through unknown territory. As parents, we *know*. We know when something is going on with our child, whether it is to do with their physical or emotional health. For most parents of autistic children, there comes a time when the fact that their child is autistic becomes crystal clear.

Autism hits a parent like an emotional asteroid; it knocks you off your feet and disrupts your equilibrium. My child is autistic; my child has autism.

The point at which this happens varies. For some parents, this is when their child is very young. Sometimes, but not always, a child diagnosed under the age of four also has some developmental delay or learning difficulties.

Some parents see their child as just 'a bit different' until the child hits a school-related milestone. This may be when they start nursery or preschool, move from Reception to Year One (around age five), or from primary to secondary school (around age 11). At these points, the differences between a child and their same-age peers make it clear that there is more to their behaviour than just quirkiness.

Your child is doing things society considers unusual. Your child is not doing certain other things children their age are meant to do. Your child is different to their peers in a way that scratches at your view of them and blurs it a bit.

You will feel a vast range of emotions as you go through this process. Here is a partial list:

- worry about your child's future and your family's future

- fear about how autism will impact your life and your family

- sadness and grief about the child you thought you would have and/or the family life you hoped for

- you may feel shame about bringing a child who is very different into your family or friendship circle as this will cause upset

- stress about how you are going to manage

- relief and validation when your gut feeling turns out to be right

- guilt because you worry that you have done something to cause your child to be autistic

- guilt because you think you should have realized much sooner that your child is autistic.

Sometimes cultural differences can impact how a parent feels as well. In some cultures, there isn't even a word for 'autism', so bringing a child with the condition into the community brings up many emotions.

Whatever you feel is unique to your journey and whatever you feel is OK. As an autistic adult, I can happily say that autism has been a massive bonus for me. It has opened doors, created opportunities and given me self-awareness and friendships I would not have otherwise had. 'Three cheers for autism!' from where I stand on my well-worn path of experience. However, I remember very well how I felt at the very beginning of this path, and I want you to know it's OK to feel less than delighted right now.

The autism journey is lifelong and has many distinct parts. The part where you are getting your head round the idea that your child is likely autistic is one. It's easy to get stuck in this phase, but moving forward out of fear and into action is essential.

Why it feels so hard

Raising an autistic child brings along with it many challenges. When your autism journey starts, you may experience some of the things listed below. For some people, several of these occur in a short space of time. This list is not meant to scare you; if you haven't encountered these issues, there's no guarantee that you will. My goal here is to help you understand why there are times when you feel overwhelmed. Throughout this book, I will provide options for managing the process and lessening the emotional impact of the situations you may encounter.

Comorbid conditions

Autism rarely travels alone. An autistic child may also have ADHD, epilepsy, dyslexia, digestive issues, hypermobility, speech and language issues and other health concerns. You may be speaking to several health professionals about your child and juggling a lot of different appointments all at once. This is a lot to manage, from the practical perspective of organizing and attending appointments to the worry you may feel about the different conditions and the stress these appointments may cause your child.

So much paperwork

Having an autistic child requires a parent to complete a lot of paperwork. Most of this paperwork – for things like applications for Disability Living Allowance (DLA), Education Health and Care Plans (EHCPs), and so on – involves you going into great detail about all of the ways your child is different to others, their struggles and the help they need. This is extremely upsetting and depressing. Completing these complex forms is even more stressful if you have a learning difficulty or struggle to communicate in writing. If you are completing these forms without help and support from understanding friends and family, this will make the process more difficult as well.

Loss of social network

As I've mentioned, what often happens for parents of autistic children is that, while they are pursuing a diagnosis for their child, or once a diagnosis is given, the people around them may not be supportive. A person might have been part of a social group of people they went to school with, but suddenly they have a child that does not fit in with the children in that group, so the parent no longer fits in either. Family members may disagree with a diagnosis or the parent's parenting style. In a very short period of time, a parent may lose their entire social network. This is extremely upsetting and isolating.

Coping with extreme behaviours

You may be dealing with extreme behaviours like violence, aggression or damage to property. For those of us who experience these kinds of things, there are few people we can talk to about this, and although it is essentially a domestic violence situation, it can't be dealt with in the same way. Many parents in this position are afraid to talk about it for fear their child or children may be taken from them because they don't understand the system.

Dealing with grief

Most parents of autistic children will need to work through some kind of grief. Some grieve for the child they thought they would have. Others grieve for the family life they hoped for. In my experience, dealing with this grief is not a linear process, and it may take a few years to come out the other side of it.

Loss of career

It is sadly very common for a parent to have to give up their job because of the demands of looking after their autistic child. For some, this can be a devastating loss as work can be an essential part of someone's identity. A person may feel totally out of control with what is happening with their child but very in control at work. When this is taken away, that can be a blow to that person's mental health.

Later life caring

You may be the child's grandparent. This comes with a whole different set of emotions and challenges, as you may not have known the child well from birth. You will have also expected your life to be very different at this point.

Relationship breakdown

It is common for couples to disagree about several things to do with their child's condition. One may disagree that the child is autistic, while the other is convinced that this is the case. The couple may intensely disagree about how to manage the child's behaviour. One parent may be simply unable to cope with the stress of raising an autistic child. The couple may have to decide to part ways for the sake of the child's wellbeing.

Single parenting

Being a single parent is not easy. When your child is autistic, there may be additional challenges. A single parent may be the autistic child's only playmate. The family may become isolated if more than one adult is required in order to access local activities and days out safely. There may be financial concerns as well.

Supporting siblings

It can be very difficult if you have more than one child. Some parents have one autistic child and one neurotypical child, and some have more than one autistic child. Every child is different and it can be hard to juggle giving attention to each of them, especially if your autistic child needs a lot of support. If you have more than one autistic child, they may have very different sensory needs to each other that can be tricky to support.

Coming to terms with 'disabled' and 'disability'

There comes a time in your child's life when you will have to start using the terms 'disabled' and 'disability' in relation to them. For example, if you apply for Disability Living Allowance (DLA), there it is, that word, 'disability', and it creates an uncomfortable, even painful lens to look at your child through. Forms like the DLA application force us to spell out our child's challenges in stark black and white.

Some local authorities have a Disabled Children's Register, and in some areas, adding your child to the register can get you some additional benefits. Here again, you are asked to think of your child in this way, 'disabled'.

Additionally, it is during this time of applying for benefits and getting your head round thinking of your child in this way that you, with the signing of a form or the sending of an email, go from being a 'parent' to being a 'carer'. There are no set criteria for what makes a person a carer other than that they have a child with additional needs.

When I started talking about this during courses and in support groups, Richard, the father of a young autistic boy, said, 'No. I am not doing this [speaking of my child as disabled]. I am not giving up hope.'[1]

For now, you may choose to use 'disabled' and 'disability' like you use your power drill or deep fat fryer. Get them out, plug them in, do the job and then put them away. You don't go round talking to people about your power drill, and you don't have to go round talking about disability, either, unless and until you are comfortable doing so.

Your own neurodivergence

You may already know you are autistic, or at some point around the time of your child's assessment and diagnosis, you may come to realize this is the case. Being an autistic parent to an autistic child can be challenging in itself as you may have different sensory needs, sleep requirements, emotional regulation methods and so on than your child does. This takes some negotiation but it can be managed. For example, my daughter is a sensory-seeking noise lover. She listens

---

1   The topic of ableism, which characterizes disabled people as inferior to non-disabled people, is a vital one for you to understand. It is, however, beyond the scope of this book. For an in-depth exploration of ableism, please read *I Will Die On This Hill* by Meghan Ashburn and Jules Edwards. (2023). Jessica Kingsley Publishers.

to things at high volume, plays piano loudly and laughs, shouts and sings constantly. I have learned to keep a supply of different headphones on hand to cope with this. I find listening to white noise (via an app) is very helpful for coping with the cacophony.

What you go through at the beginning of your autism journey is *hard*. It's OK to feel like this. Your journey is unique to you and only you can get yourself through it. Again, I'm not sharing all of these things to make you worry about what's to come. It's just that if you are already going through a few or more of these things, you may not have realized that these are the things that are making the journey feel difficult right now. It will get easier.

CHAPTER 3

Perspective Is Everything

Over the last 11 years, I have heard many parents talk about times when they were out and about and someone said something negative about their autistic child. Perhaps this little girl or boy was running around in the supermarket or being noisy in the post office, and a total stranger decided this was inappropriate behaviour. While I understand that someone saying something unpleasant about your child is upsetting, it is crucial to remember that what has been said is about the person who has said it and not about your child. Unfortunately, some ignorant people in the world feel the need to express their views no matter what the impact of those words might be. Their comments may rattle you, but please brush them off. Don't let them stick to you because they are nothing to do with you or your child.

Similarly, people have told me of situations where someone has stared at their child or given them a nasty look. I'm not discounting these experiences, but I'd like to investigate this further for your benefit.

Although my daughter can walk, we have a disability buggy for her to use when we go out. This reduces anxiety for her and keeps her safe. People often look at her in this buggy as we wheel around a park or a shop. I do not take offence at this or see their looks as negative. My perception is this: here is a large child in a large buggy; this is unusual. I believe that people who look at her while she is in the buggy are just trying to work out the physics of what they are seeing. If I'm honest, I would probably unintentionally look at this scene as well, but there is no emotion tied to this; it's a neutral observation. I believe it's the same for other people looking at her; it's just neutral, not negative.

Occasionally, I see a family with a child in a disability buggy, and my heart swells with love for them. I look at them and smile but know that my smile may be misunderstood as pity or something else. It's difficult for parents of children with additional needs to connect, especially in a typical situation like shopping and not at a special-needs-specific event.

Sometimes I am out and about with my daughter and see another child with autistic traits. This could be somewhere like a soft play or a playground, where the child is playing independently, away from the adult who brought them. Without even realizing I am doing it, I stare at this child. 'What a beautiful kid!' I think. I watch how they move and interact with others or with my child. I think, 'Aw, he's a tiptoe walker', or 'There's a deep pressure lover, like my daughter'. A few minutes pass, and I realize that if their parent is watching me watching their child, they may think my look is of judgement, rudeness or nastiness about how their child is different. In reality, mine is a look of love, affection, care and joy. I am taking in the beauty and magic of their wonderful child.

My point here is that perception is everything. If you think the world has negative, judgemental feelings about your autistic child, that is precisely what you will encounter. Your perception will be that the world is looking down on you and your child. You will regularly feel judged by the general public because that is what you expect to happen. Someone frowning to themselves over an argument they had with their partner will be misconstrued as them frowning about your child.

My daughter is very different to other children her age. She looks different, and her behaviour is that of a much younger child. A person would spend just a few minutes with her before realizing she is not neurotypical. However, in all her life, I have never once felt that anyone was looking at us in a negative way. Long ago, even before I had a child, I adopted the mindset that, 'people are inherently good'. Because I hold this view, this is the experience I have in life. People are generally kind and helpful.

If you feel that people are responding to you and your child in negative ways, you need to shift your mindset. Going through life believing the world is out to get you is not good for you or your child. It will impact your mental health, and whether or not you intend it to, it will adversely affect your child. If you believe the world is an unfriendly place, your child will come to believe that, too.

It's fair to say that there are unhelpful people in the world who feel compelled to comment on your parenting style or your child's behaviour, and their attitude of judgement and disrespect will be obvious. Sometimes, there is a case for educating these ignorant strangers, but truly, you are not responsible for this. You may choose to explain the situation to these people, or hand them an autism information card. Or you may just walk away with your head held high. It's your choice and there is no right way to manage this.

It takes practice, but any time you think you are being judged, replace the thought with a phrase like, 'people are genuinely kind' or 'people always want to help me'. The more you do this, the more you will believe it. You will be surprised at how effective this is. It may be a difficult mindset to shift if you were brought up with the idea that the world is against you. It's time to let that go as it will not help you now.

Another area where you will want to be careful of your perspective is if you believe that the people around your child are unhelpful. I have had a great deal of experience with unhelpful education and medical professionals. However, I still find that if I work on replacing a 'no one is helping my child' perspective with something more beneficial, like, 'everyone wants to help my daughter', it truly does shift my mental state into a more positive place.

Over the years I have come to understand and embrace the view that oblivion is bliss. I simply choose to believe that people are good and helpful. I also trust that everyone else has better things to do than to look at and/or judge me or my child.

I'm not making light of people being negative or unhelpful. It's my experience that a negative mindset is not conducive to a happy, productive life, and this is what I want for you.

Comparison is the thief of joy

When you have a child who is different to others, it is difficult not to compare them to other children their age. It may be the case that you have older children, and you compare your autistic child to those children when they were the same age. Or perhaps you have a younger child, so you compare that child's abilities to what your autistic child was like at that age. You may compare your child to other children in your family, other children at their school, or just random children you see when you are out and about.

You may find yourself comparing your autistic child to the non-autistic child you imagined you would have. This is a fast-track recipe for heartache and misery.

If you are comparing your child in any way, please stop. Autism is very complicated. Autistic individuals – children and adults – tend to be younger in themselves than their age on paper. Our maturity level doesn't match up to others our age, so we are always going to be different in this way. As I've mentioned, autism has various comorbidities (conditions that commonly exist alongside autism, such as ADHD, hypermobility or learning difficulties) that may cause a child to appear very different to others.

Similarly, avoid comparing your family to other families. Families with autistic children are rebels and we march to a different beat than everyone else. When you have a child with additional needs, school holidays, Christmas and birthdays can be difficult if you compare your family to others. There is no comparison. Remember that you don't know what is happening behind those happy family pictures you see on social media.

The benefits of having an autistic child

I am grateful for autism. The reasons are many.

To recap my story: having an autistic child led me to learn I am autistic, which made my life a much better, happier place. Because I have an autistic child, I set up a charity to support other parents with autistic children. This brought me incredible personal benefits. I have met thousands of wonderful people. I have made lifelong friends. I have a new career (before autism revealed itself, I worked in marketing, which I hated). I've won awards. I get to write this book for you, which is a huge honour. Truly wonderful things have happened in my life because of autism.

Raising an autistic child will teach you how resilient and capable you are. You will pull things off that you never thought possible. You will amaze yourself with your creativity, flexibility, patience and bravery. You may not believe me from where you are in your journey now, but hang in there; eventually, you will get to this point.

You will learn what is truly important in life and what is and isn't worth worrying about. Perhaps in your pre-autism life, accidentally driving the wrong way in a car park may have given you heart palpitations. Once you become a resilient badass this will be no problem. What the small stuff is in the phrase, 'don't sweat the small stuff' will become crystal clear for you.

Autism is like a patience-enhancing drug. After 13 years in this world, I have developed nearly infinite patience, not just with my child but everything. I have also developed deep compassion. Autism will help you see the world through a kinder, more interesting and colourful set of lenses. You will become more accepting of difference and disability. You will want to help other parents of autistic children if you see a family struggling when you are out and about. You will have a lot of time for the waiter who has a learning disability, or the hearing-impaired person checking you in for your flight.

You will uncover new skills you didn't know you had. I had no idea that I could write and deliver training to hundreds of people before I had an autistic child. Now I know this is my happy place. I know people who, through supporting their children, realized they had a knack for something very different to whatever they had been doing. In my friendship circle are people who dramatically changed careers. One has become an occupational therapist; there is also an inclusive workplace consultant and a few SEND (Special Educational Needs and Disabilities) law volunteers. One makes knitted sensory toys. A lot of inspiration can be found in autism parenting.

Autism doesn't discriminate. It touches every race, religion, sexual orientation and socio-economic level. This is a beautiful thing as it means the autism community is a rich and interesting resource to draw from. You will meet people you would never have met in your pre-autism life. This is a wonderful and life-enhancing experience that you can look forward to if you haven't already gotten involved with this community.

You really have to think outside the box when you have an autistic child. You will need to find creative solutions to things like making school uniform clothing more comfortable and what to put in your child's lunchbox. While at times these kinds of things are stressful, they do push us to be innovative. I feel this is a good thing.

Because you have an autistic child, you will be able to access a world of special needs play, sport and social activities. If your child attends a special school, they will have opportunities they would not have at mainstream school. Horse riding, sensory play, social skills groups and other pursuits are provided for specialist school children. Some areas have special needs playgrounds that are wonderful places. There are autism-friendly cinema screenings, autism-friendly sessions at various attractions, quiet shopping times in many large supermarkets and other shops, autism-friendly holidays, and more. These opportunities provide different ways for you to engage with your child and for your family to spend time together.

As a side note, you will develop amazing reflexes. I hadn't noticed this until I was watching a webinar by Yvonne Newbold of Newbold Hope, who mentioned this skill. Something in the way we must think on our feet when raising an autistic child also gives us the ability to catch falling objects and dodge flying ones. This is a nifty skill to have!

You also get to use disabled toilets, and I suggest you use them whenever you need to. If you are the father of an autistic girl, you can't take your daughter into the men's room with you. If you are the mother of an autistic boy over the age of about six, you may not feel comfortable taking your son into the ladies' room. You may have a child that will wander off if left outside the public toilet, so it's safest to use the disabled loos. Autism is considered to be a 'hidden disability'. More and more disabled public toilets have a sign about hidden disabilities on the door to raise public awareness of this.

Sometimes a disabled loo is a safe, quiet haven. Many years ago, I took my daughter to a soft play that was heaving with children. We went in and it quickly became overwhelming for us both. I picked her up, grabbed our shoes and got us to the disabled toilet. This was a quiet, safe place where I could get our shoes on so we could make a quick getaway.

While I'm on the subject of disabled toilets, some require a special key called a radar key. Any mere mortal can buy a radar key. You don't need to prove anything to get one. Search online for 'radar key'. They are inexpensive to buy and helpful to have. Some local authorities give them away for free, so it may be worth checking if this is the case in your area.

Another thing many of us can be grateful for is that our children will be children for longer than their same-age peers. Again, autistic individuals (both children and adults) are younger in themselves than they are on paper. Depending on your child, this may give you years more cuddles and young-childlike fun than you would have with a non-autistic child.

It's my daughter's 13th birthday tomorrow. Preparing for this has made me thankful that she is contented in herself. She does not care about fashion, hair and makeup or having the latest, most popular toys. She doesn't know social media exists. She doesn't want to try risky new things. She has a happy, simple life. I'm grateful that this is what she wants and that I can give it to her.

A beautiful garden

Autism is a permanent, lifelong condition but it is not the cause of all of your child's problems. Every autistic person has an entirely different set of traits. Your child's main difficulties may be to do with sensory sensitivities or communication. As parents, we have to support our children with the issues they struggle with.

One way to understand this is to view your autistic child as an amazing garden, and that autism is the soil in which everything in your child grows. As with any garden, there will be plants and flowers that thrive without any help and those that need support and extra nourishment.

Using this analogy, my daughter's autism 'garden' has strong, large flowers in the areas of creativity, musical talent and sense of humour. In the areas of anxiety, communication and emotional regulation, there are smaller, weaker flowers. What would your child's garden look like?

Autism is the soil for the things that make up your child's strengths and weaknesses. If you have any gardening experience, you know that soil can be good or bad, and that if you have poor soil, you can add things to it to improve it. Autism is no different. Similarly, the areas in which your child struggles just need extra support to help them along. All of your child's strengths and weaknesses rely on the 'soil' of autism. If you pull the plant out of the soil, it will die.

CHAPTER 4

Why You Need Help and How to Get It

Over the years, I have watched countless parents of autistic children try to go it alone. They might ring a helpline or ask a question on social media, get their answer and then go along their way. This person feels that they don't want to be a part of the autism community because that is not where they belong. They avoid autism support groups and socials, feeling they do not relate to the people who attend those kinds of events. They just want to get this autism thing sorted and get on with their lives.

Unfortunately, it just doesn't work like that.

It's a DIY job

It is easy – and understandable – to fall into the mindset of 'once we have the diagnosis, we'll get support/things will get better/I'll know what to do/etc'. I need you to understand one significant fact: raising an autistic child is a DIY job. There is no one book (even this one!), course or therapist that can help your child with everything. It all comes back to you and what you know at the end of the day. Even if you had the financial means to hire a great speech and language therapist, an occupational therapist, and any number of other helpful people that could help you support your child, the fact is you still have to do the work.

The work I refer to is around understanding autism. Learning about sensory processing, communication differences, how to reduce anxiety, help your child develop good self-esteem, and so on. There is no choice in this; this is something you must do. You must do this long before you have a diagnosis for your child. This process begins the moment your parental gut instinct starts telling you that your child may be, or is likely, autistic. (It is, however, important to note that if you have arrived late to this party, don't worry! There is never a 'too late' when learning about autism. The fact that you are reading this book shows you are already on the right path.)

The sad truth is that once you have had the assessment and your child has been given a diagnosis, very little help will follow. Wherever you live in the world, there's likely not much practical support available for you or your child. Unless you live in a very progressive area (and these do exist), you will not automatically be given appointments with various therapists or much of anything except perhaps a packet of leaflets about what local support is available.

Do not despair. You do not have to wait for a diagnosis of autism to support your child. Your child needs help right now (and so do you), which will feel overwhelming. Fortunately, two amazing, free resources are available to you: other parents of autistic children and autistic adults.

Many years ago, I told a mother (who also had an autistic child) at my child's school about a support group meeting that was running at a location I knew was near her home. After I mentioned the group, our conversation went like this:

'Is it just parents?' she asked.

'Yes, it is a parent support group', I answered.

'Oh', she said, 'I don't want to talk to other parents; I just want to get advice from professionals.'

'Hmm', I thought to myself. 'Who are these magical professionals she hopes to talk to?'

I don't know what ever happened to that mother, but I imagine she quickly realized that this was not an efficient (or even possible) way of getting the support she was looking for.

Your new tribe

Every parent of an autistic child knows something that someone else doesn't know. I know something you don't, and you know something I don't. Unless we talk to each other, we each hold the information we know in our little bubbles. Activities for autistic children, funding opportunities for equipment and holidays, good childcare options, where to buy seamless socks, the phone number for that great occupational therapist... there's so much we need to know to support our children. Other parents of autistic children are the top source for all of this information.

I have been working in the autism field for over 11 years. During this time, I have learned more from other parents than from any book, website, blog – or professional. Autism-related support is rarely well-advertised, whether that's meetings or playgroups or who to contact for this or that. Other parents are the ultimate source for learning about what is available to you and your child. Our community provides an endless stream of information delivered on tap for free.

A challenge is a challenge

Another thing I've seen time and time again is the parent who doesn't feel comfortable talking to other parents because they believe that the issues they are facing are not 'bad enough' to merit support. If this is you, please understand that all the problems you are facing are important and worth talking about and that other parents will welcome you and want to help you with what you are going through.

Maybe a parent at your child's school has it much worse than you. Or your neighbour is going through a really challenging time – much worse than you. Perhaps your sister's marriage is falling apart. She's got it much worse than you. It saddens me the number of times I have heard a parent say, 'I shouldn't complain; so many other people have it so much worse than me.' Often these are the parents who are going through the most challenging time of anyone I have spoken to that week.

Who is this arbiter of 'worse than/better than'? Are you struggling with something? Has something upsetting happened? Are you worried? Scared? So what if the spider in your neighbour's bathtub is much, MUCH bigger than the one in yours? Are you scared of spiders? Yes? Then just be scared.

It's OK to have a moan about things you need to have a moan about. If possible, talk to your friends, your mum and/or your partner about what you are going through instead of keeping it all bottled up. Remember, though, that you can share your worries with other parents of autistic children. I guarantee there is someone out there who will think, 'thank God it's not just me'.

RESPECT YOUR CHILD'S PRIVACY

It is acceptable and actually necessary to share the challenges you are facing in raising your autistic child with friends and family (or strangers at a support group). However, it is crucial that you respect your child's dignity and privacy if you plan to share your experiences with the wider world.

There is a growing trend for parents to share their 'autism journey' stories online in the form of blogs, YouTube and TikTok videos and other social media platforms. Some do this appropriately, writing in an anonymous way, using stock images or pictures of their child where their face is not shown and there is no identifying information. Others, however, write tell-all posts about intimate aspects of their child's life, including pictures and videos of the child. This is a terrible violation of privacy and dignity.

Only if your child is able to give you explicit permission and they have the mental capacity to understand that potentially thousands of people will see the information, pictures and videos that you share is it acceptable to share those things. The chances of a young autistic child being able to do this are very slim.

I know there are many popular and well-loved blogs and social media pages that feature images of children alongside detailed accounts of their behaviour. Some of these children lack mental capacity and have no idea that their parent is sharing such intimate details about them. I know that many parents find these kinds of blogs useful as it helps them to feel less alone. This does not make it acceptable. The same effect can be achieved while maintaining a child's privacy and dignity.

The internet is for life. You don't know what your child will be like in the future. Imagine how your child will feel if a post you have written about them at four finds its way to the people around your son or daughter when they are 14.

It is never justifiable to share the private details of your child's life in any way that identifies them. Just don't do it.

Similarly, ask your child's permission before sharing anything related to them. For example, my daughter is a prolific artist. She draws amazing pictures and makes wonderful animated films. I wanted to share some of her videos with her support worker at school, so I asked my daughter if I could do this. She said, 'no', and so I didn't.

Since she was born, we have had a social media account to post pictures and videos of my daughter for friends and family. She is a beautiful and photogenic child and for years we had a steady supply of pictures of her. As she has gotten older, she has made it clear that she doesn't like having her picture taken and she definitely doesn't like having pictures of herself shared in any way. We respect that and we don't do it anymore.

A problem shared is a problem halved

There will be things about your child's behaviour that you may feel you cannot discuss with anyone. Perhaps they smear or play with their poo or masturbate constantly. Possibly your home has damaged areas where they have put holes in the walls or broken things. Maybe you do something for your child you feel too embarrassed to tell anyone about. For example, perhaps you still brush their teeth for them, dress them, or help them use the toilet when they are far beyond the age that a parent would normally do these things.

I guarantee that thousands of other parents have experienced or are experiencing the same thing(s) as you. No matter how unusual, inappropriate, embarrassing or awkward, there is someone else out there who has been there and done that. You are never alone when you have an autistic child; there is always someone out there you can talk to. Sometimes just telling another parent about what you are experiencing, especially if you have held onto it and agonized over it for a long time, is an enormous relief.

I recall a social media conversation I happened across a few years ago, where a mum was despairing about her son's poo smearing (onto the walls, into the carpet, everywhere). Not a single person responding to her post said anything negative. Everyone who commented said they had been through the same and that it does get better. People even recommended the best carpet cleaning machines. No judgement; just help.

Beverley has an autistic child around the same age as mine. While our children are very different in many ways, they also have many similarities. Both are very anxious, so Bev and I talk about the challenges this creates. Sometimes one of us has a suggestion or idea for the other to try, but generally, we are not looking for a solution; we just need to talk about the stress of having a very anxious child.

Both of our children require us to engage in elaborate, time-consuming activities with rigid rules and expectations. These activities would be completely nonsensical and bizarre to an outsider looking in. For us as parents, these are not fun games we play with our kids – it feels more like being taken hostage. It's wonderful for us both to have someone to talk to about these scenarios. Again, neither of us is looking for advice; talking about this aspect of our children's behaviour is a relief and a release.

You are not a fraud

I can't count the number of times over the past 11 years that a parent has said to me something like, 'I shouldn't be here (getting help/attending this autism course/at this support group meeting); my daughter/son doesn't have a diagnosis yet.' If you are reading this book, but your child hasn't yet been diagnosed with autism, this does not make you a fraud. This makes you a good parent for seeking out ways to help your child.

Whether or not your child's assessment results in a diagnosis, the fact is that they are neurodivergent in some way. There is something different about their neurology. They have challenges that you can support them with. If you try a strategy recommended for autistic children and it works, then keep using it.

I promise you that no one in the additional needs parenting community will think you are a fraud, or somehow 'cheating', or getting something you don't deserve, just because your child does not yet have a diagnosis. More than half of the people you meet will be in the same situation. You are not taking up valuable space that might otherwise be taken by a parent of a child with a diagnosis. Support is there for you, wherever you are on the journey.

LISTEN TO AUTISTIC ADULTS

While other parents are the best sources for understanding what services, products and support options are available, autistic adults can give you the inside scoop on what day to day life with autism is really like.

Some parents get hung up on taking advice from an autistic adult, because 'they aren't like my child'. Remember that all autistic adults were once autistic children, and, just like you, they changed as they grew up into adulthood. Autistic adults can help you unpick why your child does the things they do and feels the way they feel.

To find blogs and social media accounts for autistic adults, search the internet for #ActuallyAutistic. This is the hashtag universally used by autistic adults to indicate that they are a bona fide autistic person.

Have a look around the internet and find a few accounts that you like the look of. Follow them, read their posts and watch their videos. The information is so insightful and is worth the well-meaning advice of 1000 non-autistic 'autism professionals'.

Another benefit of reading posts and watching videos created by autistic adults is that it may give you hope if you are worried about your child's future.

Remember: autism is a spectrum condition. You won't find *all* of the information presented by *every* autistic adult useful, so it's important that you take your time to find the people whose work you enjoy and follow them.

As your child grows up and changes, it will be important to keep updating your list of people you follow to ensure you are getting the best information to help your child.

Why we don't ask for help
Personal pride

Society tells us we have to do it all (and well). We – both men and women – are put under tremendous pressure to manage everything that life throws at us. We are constantly faced with messages like, 'You can do it all!' and 'Just do it!'. We are made to believe that anything less than perfection is unacceptable.

Judith, the mother of a teenage autistic boy, recently told me, 'If I were to give one piece of advice to a parent who is new to autism, it would be this: lower your expectations'. Judith is not talking about her child. She refers to housework, the garden and all the other bits and pieces that must be sorted. Raising children is very time-consuming, and your child's wellbeing takes priority over everything else. Sometimes, dishes will pile up in the kitchen and dusting the shelves will take a back seat. Your priorities will change dramatically.

Raising an autistic child is an unpredictable adventure with a great deal more twists and turns than a parent of a non-autistic child would encounter. Best-laid plans fall apart or morph into entirely different experiences than you were expecting. You may regularly feel overwhelmed by uncertainty and having so much to manage above and beyond what is happening in your own life with work, relationships and your own mental health.

There are many reasons we don't ask for help, but the point that repeatedly finds its way to the top of the list for parents of autistic children is pride. We don't want the people around us to know that we are not coping. We especially don't want the people around us who we have difficult relationships with to know this. If you have a tricky relationship with a parent or sibling, it can be agonizing to ask for help.

David is a single dad who has two autistic children. A few years ago, he went through a period of ill health. Emergency surgery and a subsequent infection meant he couldn't look after his children alone. David had always had a strained relationship with his mother, who did not understand autism and had always been critical of David's parenting style. When he got sick, he had no choice but to ask his mother for help. Within two days of looking after the children, David's mother began to understand the challenges he was facing and why the children did the things they did. This experience transformed the relationship between David and his mother. Since then, she has regularly looked after the children and will often stop by to help with housework.

Sometimes the people we most need help from are the hardest to ask, but it's often those people who will surprise you the most. The people around us are often desperate to help, but they don't know how or are afraid of getting it wrong. When we ask for help and provide specific ways that help can be given, we give a gift to the people in our lives who genuinely want to support us.

Dignity and privacy

Our children do some things that non-autistic children don't. They enjoy certain toys long after the given age range for that toy has passed. They partake in sensory activities that may look strange to the outside world. They may also have continence or other issues to do with health or self-care.

As parents, we want to protect our kids from the judgement of others. Autism is a misunderstood condition, and most of the general public doesn't know anything about it. This adds a layer of difficulty to asking for help because you don't want anyone to think negatively about your child based on a lack of understanding.

You also want to protect yourself from judgement. Parenting autistic children often requires you to go against the grain of how society believes children are meant to be raised. What may look like 'bad behaviour' to others is simply an autistic child's way of self-regulating. You may understand this, but your mother/sister/ friends may not.

The difficulty of delegation

As a parent of an autistic child, you will become a walking database of a vast amount of information. You will store all of this data about what your child will and won't eat, the clothes they will and won't wear, what soothes or upsets them, what their sleep (or lack of) is like, and so on. You will know all of their routines and rituals and the supplies required to carry them out.

You might avoid asking for help with childcare because you feel it is too complicated to try and explain everything your child will need while you are away. There is also the fact that your child may not cope with being looked after by anyone other than you. However, it is worth trying. You may be surprised by how well it can work with the right person.

You don't know where the help is

When my autism journey began, I had no idea where to go for help. All I had were unhelpful paediatrician appointments. I'm so happy that you are reading this book so that I can tell you where to find help. It's out there, and there is a lot of it. Without tour guides, this journey is way too hard.

Where to find support

As I've mentioned, when I first began this journey with my daughter, I didn't know there was any help at all, much less where to look for it. Over the past decade, the amount of help available for parents of autistic children has dramatically improved as awareness and diagnosis rates have increased. Below are some of the best ways to get in-person, local support.

Children's centres

If your child is under five, speak to your local children's centre. Tell them about your child's needs and find out what they have on offer for children with autism (diagnosed or suspected). Children's centres are notoriously bad at publicizing what services they offer but often have wonderful help and support. Be sure to ring them; don't rely on their website to provide the information you are looking for as you may not find it there. Our local centre was incredibly helpful for us. We were able to access sensory play sessions and meet other parents, some of whom are friends to this day! We also attended speech and language drop-in sessions and our diagnosis referral was done through one of these.

Parent carer forums

Every local authority has a parent carer forum. This is an organization that is partly funded by the council to support parents who have children with disabilities. Each parent carer forum offers a wide range of support including support groups, courses and information sessions. The support is not always autism-specific, but you can learn a lot about what other support is available in your area from your local parent carer forum. To find your local forum, search for your area and 'parent carer forum'. For example, 'Ipswich parent carer forum'.

The local offer

The Children and Families Act 2014 specifies that every local authority must have a 'local offer'. This is a website (usually within the council website) that provides details of all the support and services available for families with children with additional needs. This includes play activities and support for education, transition to adulthood and employment for children and young people with autism and other disabilities. It also includes advice for parents about benefits and how to get help from the council.

Autism and disability charities

The number of charities and community organizations that support families with autistic children is increasing rapidly. The National Autistic Society has branches in many areas. Some of these provide parent support, some provide activities for children and young people and some do both. There are also a lot of independent, local charities that offer brilliant support for families with autistic children. To find what is available in your area, search the internet for these phrases: '[your area] autism charity', '[your area] disability charity', '[your area] autism support' and '[your area] disability support'. For example, 'Woking disability charity' or 'Bristol autism support'.

How to use the internet to help your child

The internet is a great tool for finding everything from local activities and support to specific toys and devices to help your child. Here are some ways you can use the internet:

Search engines

Use search engines to find local support and help with specific issues. Searching for 'autism' and the topic (for example 'autism eating', 'autism tooth brushing' or 'autism sleep') will bring you many results. Search for what's on in your area by searching 'autism', 'autistic' or 'disability' and the name of where you live (e.g., 'autism London' or 'autism Brighton').

YouTube and TikTok

There are thousands of helpful videos about occupational therapy tips, sensory play, social stories and general autism information that may be helpful to you. There are channels run by autistic adults that may provide you with insights about autism and ways to help your child. Search for the hashtag #ActuallyAutistic.

Pinterest

You can find a huge range of sensory activities, behaviour support, links to blogs, books and other helpful resources here.

Blogs and websites

Read autism blogs – both those written by autistic adults and parents of autistic children. Search the internet for the hashtag #ActuallyAutistic to find websites and social media accounts of autistic adults. Read information on websites of autism charities or businesses. Join their mailing lists to get current information.

Social media

Join autism-related Facebook groups to get help with general and specific issues and to learn what's on. Be aware that each group has its own personality and rules. Some are positive, and some are negative. Try a few and find the ones that support you best. Use social media to find out what's happening in the world of autism – new research, interesting people, and so on. Even LinkedIn is a great place to find interesting research.

Online courses and webinars

There are now countless online course creators (me included!) running sessions on various autism topics. Search Eventbrite for 'autism' to find autism-related events, talks, training and seminars in your area, as well as virtual events and courses.

Meetup.com

Meetup.com sometimes has local autism groups.

eBay, Etsy and Amazon (including Kindle and Audible)

Search for 'autism toys', 'autism books' or 'autism sensory' to find products that may be useful. Some books can be read for free via Kindle Unlimited or may be included in your Audible subscription.

Be careful!

The internet is mostly full of excellent, helpful information but also contains a lot of dangerous nonsense. Use your common sense to navigate the information you find. If your gut feeling says 'this sounds wrong/dangerous/counterintuitive' then it probably is.

Just as 'don't go shopping when you are hungry' is good advice, so is 'don't google when you are emotional'! Do not make knee-jerk decisions (for example, putting your child on a special diet or giving them a supplement) based on what you find on the internet when you are stressed or feeling vulnerable. Please see Chapter 9 for vital information about not making your child a guinea pig.

You will spend a lot of time researching autism. This is a natural and important thing for you to do. However, be mindful of your mindset when you are doing this. Research one thing at a time and avoid going off on the many tangents that will come up while you are reading about the topic at hand. Remember: problems are much bigger at three in the morning than during the daytime.

For your research to be beneficial, it must be focused. If hours pass and you have visited dozens of links and decided to purchase several disparate books or products, this is not an effective session. Take some time away from your screen and work out what it is you are looking for. If you are after a specific answer about a specific problem, then regroup and have another look for just that issue. If what you are really after is something that will calm your anxiety and help you feel in control, you need to step away from your search for a while. You will not find what you are looking for and may end up worse off, both financially and emotionally.

A FEW WORDS ABOUT BENEFITS

Walk past any rack of newspapers and you'll see headlines about 'benefits scroungers' and 'benefits cheats'. Parents of disabled children are neither of these things. Please do not feel judged for seeking the help that you are entitled to for your child.

The government reported that there were £15 billion in unclaimed benefits in 2022. Some of this will be unclaimed Disability Living Allowance (DLA) and Carer's Allowance that parents of autistic children are not claiming because they don't feel they are eligible or they worry what other people in their lives might think.

It is very likely that your child is eligible for DLA. DLA is a non-means-tested benefit that has two components. The care component covers everything to do with looking after your child: dressing, toileting, feeding, sleeping, and so on. The mobility component deals with a child's ability to move around, follow instructions and take care around roads, cars and carparks. The care component has low, middle and high rates and the mobility component has a low and a high rate.

The form to apply for DLA is a beast. It's nearly 50 pages of documenting what challenges your child faces. This is not easy to complete.

However, if you are successful, you will get an amount of money every month that can help your child.

Autistic children are expensive. They may require specialist toys, therapies, clothing and bedding. A child may be in nappies for far longer than a non-autistic child. Your child may use a lot of water because they have a sensory need to wash a lot. Some children chew their clothing, so that it needs regular replacement. You may be doing a lot of extra washing if your child is a messy eater or if they have continence issues and you must wash their bedding more often than usual. The costs add up quickly.

You may not feel that your child needs much help or care but it may be worth having a look through the DLA form just to be sure. You may be doing quite a lot for your child that just comes naturally to you. It's often not until a parent reads through the form that they realise that all of the things they help their child with are far beyond what a parent of a non-autistic child does.

If you are successful in getting middle-rate or high-rate care for your child you will be eligible for Carer's Allowance, which is an additional benefit you can receive. You may also be entitled to grants for equipment, breaks for carers and money towards helping you in your caring role, such as massages, a new laptop or a fee for a course you want to take.

No one needs to know that you are claiming benefits. It's easy for someone who isn't walking in your shoes to judge a person who gets help for their child, especially if they don't see the child enough or understand their challenges. Claiming benefits does not make you a bad person. In fact, it may be just that bit of extra money that helps you to pursue a new career or provide something truly helpful for your child.

I've put some links for you about benefits and funding at wdisbook. com/resources.

The magic of support group meetings

It is possible that you have never in your life been to a support group, or had an issue that required one. For many people, talking about painful things with a group of strangers is the last thing they'd like to do. However, from my experience of running hundreds of support group meetings, I know that they are one of the most beneficial things you can do for your child, yourself and your family.

Support groups come in all shapes and sizes. Some are tiny, some are large. Some have cake and some don't. Some groups have speakers come to talk about specific autism-related issues. Some have crafts to do while you talk. No one group is like another, so it's worth trying a few. Each has its own personality. If you go to a group and you don't like it, please try another one. Support groups are like supermarkets – you may be loyal to one or use a few different groups.

There are many reasons why people don't want to go to support groups. The main reason is that it might be emotional. People worry that if they go to a group, they might cry, and that if they start to cry, they may never stop. It's true that you might cry. You might cry because of something happening in your life that has upset you, or you might cry in solidarity with someone else. I promise that if you cry, you will stop. I also promise that if you cry, you will feel a lot better for it. No one will judge you, and most likely the people around you will want to comfort and help you through what you are feeling.

Support groups have magical powers. As I mention elsewhere in this book, autism doesn't discriminate. This means support groups have a wide cross-section of society. You will meet interesting people you would not have otherwise met. I have made lifelong friends at support group meetings and I know many other people have, too.

An amazing transformation often takes place at support group meetings. A person will walk in, shoulders slumped, head down and tearful. After 15 minutes of talking to and getting advice from the group, they are smiling. They leave the group, standing tall, head held high and feeling confident that they have the answers to help their child with whatever's going on at that moment. It's amazing to watch this metamorphosis, and it feels great to be a part of it.

Some organizations run support groups in the daytime, some run them at night, and some do both. If you feel too tired to go to an evening support group, I urge you to give it a try. You will likely come home feeling energized and positive. You may feel you are too busy to attend a daytime group. Most groups are just an hour long, and that hour flies by. I suggest you try one and see how you find it. It may become an essential part of your life. If you work, you may be able to work out an arrangement with your employer that allows you to attend meetings for the sake of your mental health.

Virtual support groups are available, too. These are great because you don't have to leave home and attendees join from anywhere in the area or even the world. The downside is that you may not make the same kind of deep connection with attendees that you would at an in-person group. When you attend a group in person, you'll get chatting with someone while you are making a cup of tea and learn that they live in your road, or that you know their sister or that your children go to the same school. This isn't so easy in a virtual group. If a virtual group is all that is available to you, please attend. It will help you.

You can learn so much from attending support groups. Other attendees will know about autism-friendly holidays, grants, other support groups, play activities and loads of other useful things. You will learn something new every time you attend a group. I must have run over 300 support groups, and I learned at least one new thing at every one of them.

When you attend a support group meeting, you'll quickly realize you know more than you think you do. Someone will need help and you will know the answer. This will be a huge boost to your confidence. Helping people feels great and is addictive!

Setting up a support group

When I started running support groups, I had no idea what I was doing. I had never been to a support group, much less organized one. I am a shy introvert. Having to talk to strangers is hard for me. However, I knew that there was a need to bring people together that wasn't available in my area, and I was compelled to do something to change this.

I started the easy way, by organizing a pub meetup group. This meant that there was no meeting room to hire, set up or clean up;

people came along and bought their own drinks. We soon outgrew the pub, though, and had to move on to a church hall.

At this point, my mental health was poor. I was passionate about helping people but getting through the days was like walking through molasses. When there was a group I had to run, I always felt like I could not possibly do it, could not possibly go and open the door, put out the chairs and make the tea. As I was the only one with the keys to the building, there was no choice but to put one foot in front of the other and go and run the group. Every single time, without fail, something amazing happened: at the end of the group, I felt fantastic. Every single time. There is just something about helping people that feels great. If I can do it, anyone can.

The process for setting up a support group is too lengthy to share in this book. So passionate am I for you to do this that I have created a video for you that explains the process. You can find this at wdisbook.com/resources.

Running support groups utterly changed me as a person. Before I started doing this I was an extremely anxious person. I struggled with depression. Through running support groups, my nearly constant anxiety and depression disappeared, only to return for very short periods a few times a year. There truly is magic in running and attending support group meetings.

Talking to friends and family about autism

This is possibly the most emotional part of talking about autism. Telling close family and friends that your child is autistic is hard. We can feel like we have failed somehow or done something wrong. Of course, we haven't, but it is very normal to feel like this. Once you tell people, your world will change. It may make you feel quite vulnerable and a little exposed. Remember though that we are talking to those people so that they can help us, and hopefully, we will be more bonded to them. As I've said, these conversations can bring you closer to the people in your life.

Before you have conversations about your child's autism, plan what you are going to say and think through potential counterarguments. Discuss the core issues of autism, such as problems with communication, social skills, repetitive behaviours and the need for routine. Explain how these things affect your child and remind the person of times when they have seen these issues in action. Share with the person you are talking to that these behaviours are not intentional or even controllable, but part of your child's neurological makeup.

Bear in mind that waiting until after your child has received a diagnosis to speak to friends or family may cause upset. You have had a long time to think, read and learn about autism. The person you are telling is getting this information for the first time when you tell them, and it can be a lot to take in. Be compassionate and patient. Just like we must adjust to a 'new life', so may the person you are telling. They may need time to get their head round the information and grieve for what they thought they would have. The fact that the issues your child has may not be obvious to the person you are speaking to may add a layer of difficulty for them in terms of understanding the diagnosis.

Be sure to focus on the positives. Talk about the strengths your child has, such as an amazing memory or attention to detail. (These may or may not be related to autism, but it may help to share these traits.) Clarify that you have had your child assessed because it will bring them help in the future. Point out that a diagnosis is quite difficult to get and is only given when a child is truly autistic.

The person you are speaking to may ask what caused your child's autism. They may also think it is something that can be cured. Be prepared with the facts. Also, be prepared for the fact that well-meaning friends and relatives may send you articles or books about autism cures and amazing 'recovery' success stories. Thank them and move on.

Give friends and family members ideas for how they can help you. As I've mentioned elsewhere, sometimes the people around us yearn to help us but they don't know how or worry they will offend us somehow. Give them some clear ideas of how they can support you.

Grandparents and other relatives may need help interacting and playing with your child. It may be difficult for older relatives to understand your child's differences, or that your son or daughter may like playing with toys designed for children much younger than they are. Teach them how to talk to your child and what your child likes to do.

The people in your life that you talk to about your child being autistic may react in a different way than you expect, for better or worse. Carly's mum, upon hearing the news of her grandson's diagnosis, said, 'Oh, thank heavens! I have thought for years that he is autistic but didn't want to upset you.' Ewan's parents, on the other hand, reacted badly to the news at first, but then went out and bought every book about autism that they could find and became very supportive of their grandchild.

There will be people in your life that will outright reject your child's diagnosis. Please do not take this personally. As I've said, most people don't know anything about autism. People fear what they don't understand. Others may think they understand autism (based on a film they've seen or an article they read in a newspaper) and don't agree with your child's diagnosis because it doesn't line up with their view of the condition. Some people you speak to will simply find the idea of your child being autistic too much to bear. These are not easy situations. Again, patience and a cool head will prevail here.

There are a lot of books, videos and other resources you can use to explain autism to the people in your life. Visit wdisbook.com/resources to learn about these.

As I've mentioned elsewhere in this book, it is unfortunately common for people to lose friends and become estranged from relatives when they share the news that their child is autistic. This can be devastating; people you have known all of your life no longer wish to see you. Every situation is different and I don't have any great advice here. It may just take time for people to come round, or you may simply need to move on and find other, better and more accepting friends.

Similarly, you may choose to disassociate with friends who have non-autistic children because it's just too painful to be around them.

I was part of an NCT group when I was expecting my daughter. Although I kept in touch with them for the first few years after our children were born, the difference between my daughter and the other children was vast. It was just too painful to have to explain her differences and watch the other children run rings around her.

My friend Caroline has a relative that she has to see but who doesn't understand or accept her autistic son. She chooses to see that person on her own for a coffee instead, thus avoiding any need to explain or defend her son. Sometimes, we just have to find a way forward with the people around us who just don't 'get it' and for whom there is no chance of changing their viewpoint.

You will likely go through a period of friendship flux, where your current social circle shifts around the changes in your life. Some friends will stay and some will go. You will also begin to make new friends in the autism world and each of these will be a life preserver, sounding board and safe place to land all in one. Sometimes in life, the things and people that no longer serve us drop away and make room for new, more beneficial things and people. This may be a very difficult phase for you, but you will get through it.

CHAPTER 5

The Importance of Assertiveness

Most of us come into parenting an autistic child as shy and timid individuals who don't want to make a fuss or upset anyone. You will quickly realize that this is not the way forward. Shy and timid does not win any races in Autismland. You must learn to stand up and become an effective and successful advocate for yourself and your child. You must also lead by example – your advocacy teaches your child how to advocate for themselves.

Assertive vs. aggressive

It's easy to confuse 'assertive' with 'aggressive'. Assertiveness is a quiet power. It's a way to communicate honestly and respectfully to get what you want and need in your life and for your child. Being assertive means respecting yourself by standing firmly by what you believe is right. You will gain the respect of others by not backing down.

Aggression, on the other hand, will not get you far. Going into a situation with the school or your partner or the paediatrician all guns blazing will only have a negative effect. You will not get what you want by raising your voice, being physically intimidating, or bullying the person with daily calls or emails. I know this can be difficult. I have been in many situations where it's taken a huge effort not to shout at the Special Educational Needs Co-Ordinator (SENCO) or paediatrician. Being aggressive is detrimental. You may actually find yourself banned from speaking to the professionals you need to speak to the most.

The other danger of being aggressive is that often when we get angry, what finally sets us off is not what we are actually angry about. If we are not careful, we can end up taking out our rage about the wait for the autism assessment on a teacher or someone else when it has nothing to do with them. During one extremely stressful and frustrating period, I found that I had to get help with anger management, and you may want to think about this, too. Most parents of autistic children are very angry people, due to how unfair the SEND system is and how hard we have to fight to get support and help for our children.

Why we have to be assertive

As parents of autistic children, we have a lot more to sort out than parents of non-autistic children. We must teach our children so many things and support them in gaining independence. We have to advocate for them with health and education professionals. We must educate the people around our child, including family members and friends. Some situations require us to appeal a decision or push back on something to get what is needed for our son or daughter.

Gaining assertiveness needn't feel overwhelming. It is like a muscle; the more you use it, the stronger it will become. You can build your assertiveness muscles by pushing back against all sorts of things – it doesn't even need to be about your child. For example, you could start by asking for a different table in a restaurant or complaining about poor service you've received. Say 'no' when you need to; don't take on more than you can manage just because it suits the person asking you to do so.

THE BENEFITS OF BEING ASSERTIVE

- *You'll get more of what you want, more often.* If you don't ask you don't get. The best way to get what you want – whether that is a tangible thing or an emotional benefit – is to ask for it.

- *You won't get what you don't want.* Being assertive and saying 'no' when you need to will stop you getting things you don't want.

- *It will improve your self-esteem and confidence.* Confidence, self-esteem and assertiveness all feed off each other so improving one will help you with all three.

- *It will reinforce your self-worth.* Being assertive is about respecting yourself. Whether you are saying 'yes' or 'no', as long as you are in line with your values then you will respect your self-worth.

When you first begin to flex your assertiveness muscles, the people around you won't like it. You are behaving very differently to how you have done over the time they have known you (whether that's a few months or decades). Disturbing the status quo makes people uncomfortable. Work through the discomfort. Your assertiveness will reap rewards by getting what is needed for you and your child, thus improving their happiness and wellbeing. These rewards will build your confidence and encourage you to keep going.

The power of 'why?'

A great way to practise assertiveness is to ask, 'why?'. 'Why?' is a small but powerful question. For example:

- Why can't my child have this reasonable adjustment at school?

- Why can't we have the first appointment of the day?

- Why can't the GP meet us in the waiting area?

- Why can't we arrive 15 minutes before everyone else?

- Why can't my child eat the food we brought from home when the rest of us are ordering meals?

Once you start asking 'why?', keep at it like a dog with a bone. You will have conversations like this:

> You: 'Why can't my child have ear defenders at school?'
>
> School: 'Because it will be disruptive to other children.'
>
> You: 'Why will it be disruptive to other children?'
>
> School: 'Because he will have to ask for them each time they are needed.'
>
> You: 'Why will he have to ask for them each time they are needed? Why can't he get them himself?'
>
> School: 'Because then every child will be wanting to get things out of their bags.'
>
> You: 'Why would my child getting something out of his bag make other children want to do this?'

Unless there is a real reason why something is impossible, the answers from the person you are 'whying' will get increasingly bizarre. Eventually, they will give up in defeat and realize that they genuinely don't have a good reason why you can't have what you want. Sometimes the answer to your 'why?' will be something like 'we have always done it that way', because the person you are asking simply doesn't have an answer.

Get in with the thick skin

To successfully parent a child with additional needs, you must develop a thick skin. Being assertive will help you do this. The more you use your assertiveness, the stronger and more capable you will feel, and what other people think of you will matter less and less. The most valuable piece of advice I have ever been given is this: *what other people think of me is none of my business.* Ingrain this in your mind. Write it on sticky notes and put them around your home. Visit wdisbook.com/resources for a card you can print, laminate, and keep in your purse or wallet. Never forget that what other people think of you is none of your business. Just focus on the needs of yourself, your child and your family

Boundary setting 101

You will need to set firm boundaries to protect your child, your family and yourself. Boundaries also help to maintain a calm home atmosphere. Assertiveness is crucial for boundary setting.

The boundaries I am talking about include things like how friends and family speak to you about your child and ensuring that everyone in your household follows key rules. Boundaries are also great for helping your child understand that there are limits for things like how much they can eat or how much time they spend online.

In my experience, you can't ease into boundary setting. You must decide what is needed, set a boundary, make the boundary clear to all involved and stick to it. The key is to set realistic boundaries, and provide the people involved the tools and information needed to help them adhere to them.

Setting boundaries with your child

Autistic children (and adults) rarely present as the age they are on paper. A 12-year-old girl may at different times act like an eight-year-old, a five-year-old, or a 16-year-old. Our children take a very, very long time to develop solid emotional regulation skills so it's crucial for us as parents to understand this and be patient. Every child – autistic or not – goes through periods of testing boundaries. Their behaviour is intended to push us: 'I've done this awful thing! Do you still love me?' It's hard not to punish what society considers to be 'bad behaviour', for example a child who has damaged property. It's crucial to work out what is behind that behaviour first. We'll come on to this in Part Two.

I went through a phase with my daughter where she was constantly demanding food. I set a boundary around how much she would eat at meals and for snacks, and I created a clear visual guide for this, with each meal attached to the visual guide with Velcro.

When the meal or snack was finished, it would come off the page. At the end of the day when all of the meals and snacks had been removed from the page, eating was finished. The guide was attached to the door of our living room so that it was visible at all times for her. She quickly understood the boundaries and the problem was solved.

Alongside this, I added some extra sensory activities in, like playing with rice and using a skin brush on her arms and legs. Sometimes a child overeats simply because they are craving more sensory stimuli, and this was the case for my daughter.

You can use things like timers or parental control apps to set boundaries as well. We use coloured sand timers where each colour is a different amount of time, for example, blue is one hour and red is 20 minutes. To be honest, it took us a few years to get the hang of using these timers but now we use them all day, every day. One black timer (30 minutes) until bed. One purple timer (15 minutes) until it's time to get dressed. The timers are very visible and easy for kids to understand as they can literally watch the passing of time.

Another useful home boundary-setting tool is to use a device like an Echo Dot or Google Nest to create routines and make announcements to various parts of your home. This has worked incredibly well in my house, as it's Google and not Mummy nagging to do this or that.

Strategies for boundary-setting success

- Set clear boundaries and be consistent – even when it's hard.

- Become the person they trust most in the world by being consistent, reliable and supportive.

- Be a good role model – no 'do as I say not as I do' here.

- Be creative – find other ways of saying 'no', for example, 'the bank says I can't buy that toy for you'.

- Give choices instead of demands, for example, 'what do you want to do first, brush your teeth or put on your pyjamas?'.

- If you have to say 'no', explain why.

- Empathize with your child; put yourself in their shoes.

- Remember: you are the adult and you are in control of your emotions where your child isn't or is struggling to be; don't fight fire with fire.

It's often much easier to give in to a child's demands than to say no. However, being inconsistent will cause anxiety for your child as more often than not they will thrive on predictability and knowing what the rules are makes them feel safe. You need to be consistent, not just by setting clear boundaries but by being present for them. Be reliable – meet your promises and do as you say you will. This will make being assertive with your child much easier as they will come to learn what your expectations for them are.

If you have a partner who shares the parenting with you, make sure you work together and are 'singing from the same hymn sheet'. You don't want to get into a situation where your child is able to play one of you off against the other. If you are the boundary-setter in your house, be sure to clearly explain boundaries and the reasoning behind the boundaries to everyone involved in the care of your child. This may require some negotiation to ensure everyone understands and follows the plan consistently.

Other things to consider are that your child may struggle with facial expressions, tone of voice and body language – not just reading other people's but their own. You might feel that your child is being rude to you from the tone of their voice but that may not necessarily be the case. If you are angry, your child may laugh at you, not because they find it funny, but they don't understand that you are upset.

Being assertive with your child is a very complex subject as there are so many things to consider, for example: your child's age, cognitive ability, the situation and the many possible reasons behind their behaviour. The most important thing is to start. It may be painfully difficult at first to set and stick to boundaries but perseverance will pay off in the long run.

Setting boundaries with everyone else

With friends and family, setting boundaries may be more difficult and more emotional. The bottom line is that if someone in your life is doing something that is upsetting you, you need to work out how you can stop or limit them from doing this. The rest of this chapter will help you with this.

DEALING WITH COMMON SILLY THINGS PEOPLE SAY ABOUT AUTISM...

'In my day, we didn't have autism'

Autism has always been around. It just wasn't as well understood as it is now. There are not more autistic individuals now, just better assessment and diagnosis, especially for girls and women.

'Why do you want to label her?'

Diagnosis will help my child gain better access to help, therapies and support. It will help her when she is older as well, to get help at college and work.

'You need to make him eat/talk/etc.'

He will do these things in his own time. He has sensory/developmental issues that physically prevent him from doing them now.

'She just needs discipline; you're too soft'

Autism is a neurological difference that affects how people think and act. My child needs love, care and understanding; discipline is not the answer.

'But we're all a bit autistic!'

We are not. Autism is a diagnosable, neurological condition with specific traits. The Little Black Duck, an Australian autism wellbeing service, gives the helpful analogy that being 'a little bit autistic' is like being 'a little bit pregnant'. A person may have indigestion and swollen feet (some symptoms of pregnancy) but this does not make them pregnant.

'My child does that, too'

People generally say this in a well-meaning way, to help you feel better about what is going on in your life. They don't realize that although their child may indeed do something similar, it's not to the extreme level your child does whatever the thing is.

Disruptive parenting

There is a term used in business, generally about a technological business or innovation, that refers to a way of working that goes against the grain but is still very successful. The term is: *disruptive*.

As parents of autistic children, we have to quickly move past our timidness into what I call 'disruptive parenting'. Disruptive parenting means doing very nearly the opposite of what you have always done before and what society tells you is expected. For example: going out in the rain, staying indoors on sunny days. Disruptive parenting means saying 'no'. As in:

'No, Mum, we will not be coming to yours on Christmas Day because it's just too much for Elliot.'

'No, Sis, please don't wrap up all of your gifts for Jennifer because she finds surprises very stressful.'

'No, we won't be having a birthday party for Gregory because he simply doesn't want one.'

'No, Nan, please don't burn those scented candles when Amanda visits because they give her a headache.'

So: *no*. Disruptive parenting is about finding your backbone and your thick skin. You can use it everywhere your child goes – relatives' homes, school, church, Scouts and with your neighbours. The more you use it, the easier it gets, the happier your child will be, and the more confident you will become. It's also about parenting your way, not your mother's way or your friend's way or the way the other mums at the school gate parent their kids. *Your* way.

Disruptive parenting gives you a licence to stand up for yourself, your child and your family. Your child will wear what is most comfortable for them, even if they are 14 and what they want to wear is a Tigger onesie. Your child will eat what is least offensive to them. They will do whatever they want for their birthday. My daughter loves blowing out candles on her birthday. She's not into eating cake but we'll light the candles and she'll blow them out until they melt everywhere and we throw the cake away. That's what she likes so that's what she gets. You can do whatever works for your family during school holidays. You can stay indoors on warm, sunny days. You don't have to do what anyone else does.

I used to live in a road full of terraced houses where in almost every house there was at least one if not three or four non-autistic children. Every year, my neighbours would have a street party. Everyone would open their doors, the kids ran around everywhere, there was a bouncy castle and a table full of cakes for a Bake-Off style contest. For about 257 reasons, there was absolutely no way we could participate in this. The first few years, this awful event would roll around and we'd feel so uncomfortable, hiding inside while everyone else was outside having all this fun. After that, we made a note of the date and went away for that weekend. Doing what was right for our family felt good and was far more fun than being at home. I don't know if it upset any neighbours but it didn't matter.

Start small

Disruptive parenting takes time to get the hang of. It is not automatic or comfortable to go from being someone who doesn't make a fuss to someone who fiercely protects their child's wellbeing, even when this inconveniences or upsets someone. The good news is that, just like with assertiveness, it is possible to ease into disruptive parenting. Take baby steps. Try changing playdate plans with a friend or telling your mother you will arrive later than initially agreed for a family dinner. Start saying 'no' when you need to. Practise at every opportunity.

You know in your heart that you need to do this. You will have already had some disastrous family get-togethers or holidays that didn't work because your child could not cope with whatever was going on. You may be struggling with your child's school and know you need to put your foot down to get them to support your child in the way they should. Disruptive parenting is the way forward for you to get things done.

It's fun!

Disruptive parenting will delight your inner teenage rebel. It gives you the chance to put two fingers up to the way the world thinks you should parent your child. Rewarding for this and punishing for that? No thanks. Expensive birthday parties? Nope. My friend Sonja and I had a giggle recently when we were talking about what we have for Christmas dinner. 'We just have pigs in blankets', she told me. 'We realized that of all the things people eat for Christmas dinner, that is what we like the most, so that is what we are having.' For Christmas at my house, my daughter eats plain pasta and the adults eat Japanese steak and cheese. Sometimes we don't even have Christmas on Christmas Day but on the 23rd or 27th or some other day. We are such rebels!

If the idea of disruptive parenting feels uncomfortable to you, why is that? If the reason is because you don't want to look different, please think this through. Our lives *are* different to those of parents with non-autistic children. It's best to go with the flow here. Embrace different.

Being assertive with education professionals

Getting support for your child at school and dealing with education professionals will be one of the most stressful things you will encounter. Knowing how to get what you need for your son or daughter is vital. You need to plan what to say and how to say it.

Dealing with education issues will make you angry. We all need a moan once in a while. However, if that moan is not followed by assertive action, it won't help your child get better care. You can get angry and rant about how this or that is wrong and unfair, but it's best to calm the anger and channel your efforts into helping your child.

If you want professionals to take you seriously and listen to what you say (and help you and your child), you must behave like a professional yourself. This means doing your research, preparing your case, standing tall and presenting information calmly and firmly. I'm not being patronizing; you want and need them to help you! Attitude is everything.

If you want to be taken seriously, acting in an aggressive manner will put people on the defensive and make them far less likely to want to help you. I know it's emotional – we are talking about your child. However, emotions must be set aside as much as possible. Before you go into the meeting or make the phone call, try a visualization exercise. Imagine you are made of steel, or that you put on a suit of armour, or that you are in a protective bubble where nothing can touch you. Sounds silly, but it works. If you are spiritual or religious, ask a higher power or God to give you the words to say.

Before the meeting or call, work out the answers to these questions:

- What is your desired result?

- Why do you want that?

- Is this a reasonable request?

- Is it the school's legal obligation to do what you are asking?

- How will your child benefit?

- If it's a school issue, how will the school benefit?

- When do you expect the issue to be resolved?

Having clear answers to these questions in mind will help you to get what you want.

Be sure to respect the other person's time. If your child's teacher can't talk during school drop off or pickup times, make an appointment at a time convenient for both of you. Sometimes this takes a bit of reminding, but don't give up. If for some reason you are unable to make the appointment, be sure to let them know and reschedule.

Don't be the person who goes into every new situation with their child with a long list of their child's needs and requirements. It's hard not to do this, especially when it comes to school. Providing a teacher with a 12-page dossier about your child won't make you very popular. It is often better to drip feed information. Explain the most crucial things and then work from there. Remember – assertiveness is a quiet power.

If you want to be heard, appearance is important. I know we are often exhausted, and just getting out the door for the school run can be a job. However, it will make a difference if you make an effort with your appearance when meeting face to face with professionals. You don't need to go in suited and booted, but dress as you would if you were having a meeting with your bank manager. Have a shower, and wash your hair. I'm not being patronizing. This will not only help you to appear more credible but it will help you feel more confident.

Be sure to take good, clear notes during the meeting. You may even want to ask if you can record the conversation using your phone to remember what was said. (They may say no, and you'll need to respect that decision.) Write down everything you can during the conversation. Ideally, have a friend or relative come along and take notes for you, so you can focus on what's being said.

During your conversation, decide on dates for when the action points discussed (both things that they must do and that you must do) need to be done. After the meeting, write up your notes and email them to everyone who was present at the meeting and copy in the Headteacher. Write out what was discussed and what you understand the next steps will be and include the dates you agreed on.

Keep tabs on those agreed dates. If there is something for you to action, let the person you are dealing with know when you've done your bit, and gently remind them if the date is getting close to when they are meant to have delivered on their promises.

The ideal scenario with whoever you are talking to about your child is that you are working in partnership with them. Again, this is about being assertive and not aggressive. If you take the approach of 'following my advice will make your job/life easier', you will have more success than demanding that they do this or that. Express very clearly what's in it for them – how will they benefit from following your guidance? If you can work alongside and not against the professionals caring for your child, you can work progressively through issues instead of fighting a battle.

It's important to be realistic when asking the school for help. It's realistic to ask for and expect social skills support for your son or daughter. It's not realistic to expect the school to provide a private room for your child to work in every day. If you can't get what you want (and it's not something that is a statutory obligation required by law), don't shoot the messenger. Remember that raising an autistic child is a DIY job. Ask other parents what they did in a similar situation. Find a book or course on the issue your child needs help with. Hire a private speech and language therapist, occupational therapist or social skills trainer. I am not being flippant here – sometimes we must do and pay for things ourselves.

Being assertive with healthcare professionals

The NHS can feel like a very mysterious and frustrating entity when you have an autistic child. The things your child most needs – an autism assessment, speech and language therapy, occupational therapy and mental health support – are often painfully difficult to get.

Assertiveness is especially important when dealing with health professionals. Most GPs, nurses and consultants have surprisingly little training or understanding of autism. A referral for your child to any particular department is generally done in the same way as a referral for any person to any department, with no thought given to sensory or other needs. In my experience, and the experience of many parents I have worked with, autism is not taken very seriously.

If you feel that your child needs a particular service, ask your GP for a referral. Depending on what you need, the school may also refer. For example, if your child needs an autism or ADHD assessment, or help from CAMHS (the Child and Adolescent Mental Health Service), the school can put in a referral for you.

You may need to be assertive to get this referral made. If your child behaves very differently at school than they do at home, the person you are asking may fob you off because they don't believe there is an issue. You may be able to self-refer to the service, depending on your area.

Similarly, there are medical professionals who will attribute just about any issue to autism. When my daughter was nonspeaking, I could not get speech and language help for her because it was thought that her lack of speech was simply part of autism. Mental health issues can also be dealt with this way. You really do have to push to get things done.

Once a referral is made you may have to wait a long time for your child to be seen. Again, assertiveness is useful here as you may need to ring up to find out where your child is on the waiting list and if they can be seen any sooner. When your child is seen by a speech therapist, occupational therapist or CAMHS staff, provide that person with clear information and what you hope to achieve. It may be the case that your child is only allotted a few appointments, or is discharged before even being seen. If you feel this is not enough, push back to get more support for your child.

It really shouldn't have to be like this. I shouldn't have to tell you how to get help, because the help should be given automatically. Sadly, funding for the NHS has been cut to the bone and beyond and so we do have to fight to get what our children need. There is an American saying that says, 'the squeaky wheel gets the grease'. Be the squeaky wheel with medical professionals.

Professionals are people, too

When I was a child, I thought that my teachers lived in the school I went to. I believed they existed just for me and the other students. I had no concept of them having lives or families outside of school. As parents, we are sometimes guilty of this, too. If we feel a professional has failed our child, it's easy to forget that they have a life, too, that may be affecting their work. They may have a difficult partner. They might be recovering from the death of a parent or a close friend. They may even have a child with a disability. The point I am trying to make is that teachers, medical and government staff are humans, too, and as such, sometimes we must give them the benefit of the doubt.

On an organizational note, I'm sure you have already realized that having a child with autism generates a massive amount of paperwork. It's essential to keep everything together so you can find it when needed. Invest in some storage boxes or lever arch files. Keep subjects (e.g., 'Diagnosis paperwork' and 'Education paperwork') in clearly labelled files or folders. If that's too complicated, do what I do and just keep it all in one lidded box. Also, create an email folder to hold all your education-related emails, both sent and received. Doing this will make it much easier to find the reports and other 'evidence' you need when you are completing forms and asking for help. It's easier to be assertive when you have all the facts on paper, and you can find things when you need to.

THE ART OF COMPLAINING

If, despite your best efforts, someone is not helping your child:

Find out the complaints procedure for the school/local authority/ government department. It should be on their website, otherwise, email or ring and ask for it. Follow it precisely; don't be tempted to jump to the last bit (where you are speaking to the highest authority on the list) as you will be told to start at the beginning. Usually, the stages are:

1. Complain to the immediate person who is not helping you – the teacher or the department.

2. If you do not get the outcome you seek, escalate to the next level up – the head or the local authority.

3. If you do not get the outcome you seek, carry on up the chain.

Complaining is underrated. Every government department that looks after your child has a complaints procedure that is clear and straightforward. Complaining is just a business transaction and must not be feared.

I have complained to two different schools on behalf of my child. I was successful in both cases, and I feel this was because I had kept all of the emails and paperwork from the schools, so I could reference dates and things that happened. I followed each school's complaints procedure to the letter. I was calm and professional with the people I dealt with (though I did not feel calm and professional inside!).

It's unfortunately the case that if you have an issue with your child's school, it may take a long time to sort out. By following the complaints procedure, you will move things forward and possibly find interim solutions, such as moving your child to a different class with a different teacher (if this is appropriate) or getting them some of the support they need in school.

Also consider writing to your MP or councillor about what is happening. A letter from them may be just the push that is needed to get things sorted.

Assertiveness will help you get what you need for your child and for yourself. Becoming an assertive, disruptive parent may require some uncomfortable behaviour changes for you. Most things worth doing require effort and aren't easy. Building up your assertiveness muscles will be incredibly beneficial for you and your family.

CHAPTER 6

How to Look After Yourself

We can get so wrapped up in looking after our child that we forget to look after ourselves. We forget to eat, or to eat well. We don't take time to collect our thoughts. If we are not careful, we can forget who we are and what we want.

I don't need to tell you that learning that your child is autistic hits hard. Unless you are already aware of autism and know that it runs in your family, the news that your son or daughter is autistic will throw you off balance. Life is not going to be how you thought it would be. Your child may walk a very different path to the one you were expecting.

I can tell you that it is entirely possible to live well, both mentally and physically, while raising an autistic child. What that looks like for you will be very personal and will require effort on your part. You will need to hang on to your sense of self and discover what you need to thrive.

It will take time for you to assimilate the billion things you have to get your head round in order to support your autistic child. It's overwhelming at first but in time you will understand how all the different facets come together. Your confidence will grow, and you will settle in yourself. After 13 years of looking after my daughter and 11 years of looking after a lot of other parents I have seen this happen over and over. Most parents of autistic children follow the same trajectory, which looks something like this:

Autism journey begins

↓

Worry and fear

↓

More worry and fear

↓

Waiting for assessment; still more worry and fear

↓

Overwhelm due to the sheer volume of
information required to support child

↓

Try this, that and the other thing; nothing works

↓

Start connecting with other parents

↓

Try something new; it works!

↓

The next thing works, too!

↓

Confidence grows

↓

Diagnosis is given

↓

Begin to feel less isolated

↓

Find the best sources of information

↓

Settle into autism journey

My point is that if you are feeling scared and isolated now, in time you will feel better. The key to this happening is to do the work. Read books, watch videos of autistic adults talking about their lived experience, meet other parents, do the research and try a lot of different things to help your child with the things they find challenging. It's not easy, but then parenting in general isn't easy.

A lot of people have the idea that self-care is all about massages and manicures. Those are nice things, but self-care is about far more than occasional treats and pampering. True self-care is about how you look after yourself on a daily basis in order to stay healthy and happy.

Your self-care routine is unique to you, and may take a bit of time and trial and error to work out. Think of it like choosing items from a buffet of delicious and delightful things that make you feel good. If you try something new that you don't like, you can simply replace it with something else from the buffet.

Self-care isn't selfish. If you are not physically and mentally well, you will find it difficult to effectively manage the care of your child. This chapter is not meant to be preachy. It's intended to help you work out what a good self-care regime looks like for you, and it offers ways you can incorporate some new ideas that can help you feel your best, physically, emotionally and mentally.

What are you in control of?

A huge amount of energy can be wasted worrying about things you are not in control of. You *are* in control of yourself – your actions, your words, your thoughts, opinions, responses, how you look after yourself, etc. You *are not* in control of everyone else – their actions (or lack of), responses, etc. This includes the school, the health service, your child, your partner, your mum, your neighbour, etc.

It's crucial that – as early as possible – you come to understand what you are and are not in control of. Assertiveness is great but if you are pushing against something you have no control over it will be pointless and exhausting. Self-care is something you are entirely in control of. It is just for you, and you can choose how you want to look after yourself.

Good food

I honestly believe that eating well is the best self-care around. What this looks like for you is very personal. I love to cook and even though I am on my own most of the time, I enjoy cooking for myself. It feels like I am giving myself a big hug when I sit down with a plate of healthy, well-made food. I put on a lot of weight around the time I learned that my daughter was autistic. That is coming off slowly, but it's required me to cut out sugar and increase the amount of fruit, vegetables and good quality meat that I eat.

You may not be into cooking and that's OK. Supermarkets are offering more healthy convenience options, such as pre-cut vegetables and pre-seasoned meat. If finances allow, you could invest in a cookery subscription that sends you a box with ingredients and recipes each week. There are scores of basic cookery books available plus loads of recipes online for anything you might like to cook.

Eating well has many benefits. Now that I've removed a lot of junk from my diet, I feel better and I'm able to think more clearly. I'm less stressed and my sleep is much better, too.

Exercise

I really hate exercise. It's just not my thing. However, it must be done. Although I live in a lovely part of the country and am surrounded by walking paths, I don't like to walk on my own. Instead, I ride a recumbent bike several times a week and do online dumbbell workout videos. This works for me.

If you are not an exercise person, you will need to find something that works for you, too. You may love exercise and already have this part of your life sorted with running, the gym or Zumba. However, if you don't, please start thinking of ways you can get a bit of exercise into your life. I find that getting up early (I know, this is a really off-the-wall idea, isn't it!) and getting exercise in before I have a chance to talk myself out of it works best.

A note about alcohol

It's very common in online forums for parents of autistic children for people to joke about drinking. 'I'll be heading straight for the gin after I get this form finished!' and 'I'll definitely be treating myself to wine after this day is over' are the kinds of things people often say in our world. If you are prone to drinking, please be careful. It's very easy to fall into the bad habit of drinking too much as a way to cope with the stress you are going through. While it will help you in the moment, it won't do you any favours in the long run. If you find yourself drinking more than you should, please think about what other things you may be able to do to calm yourself.

I love wine and would happily drink every day. However, even a small amount makes it impossible for me to do anything productive. Also, as a single mum, drinking is just a bad idea. I now don't keep wine in the house and drink very, very rarely. Instead of drinking in the evenings, I unwind in other ways, by reading or listening to music (child allowing). If alcohol is a problem for you, please address this for your good health.

Don't lose your self

It's difficult for parents not to lose themselves in their children. This is especially true for parents of autistic children. There's so much to learn and do, we can easily forget about our own needs. Doing things you enjoy and spending time with people who energize you is an important part of self-care.

In Chapter 13 I talk about how you can help your child learn more about themselves. All of those activities are useful for you, too. When I sat down and started writing out my favourite things, scents, places and people I was surprised that they weren't what I thought they were. For example, I had always thought I had a sweet tooth but in fact, I prefer sharp and savoury things like red wine, dark chocolate, strong cheese, lemon and olives.

Writing out your favourite things will help you to ensure that you do them. Do you love the ocean? Make sure you go there at least once a year, if not more often. Do you love the smell of lavender?

Buy a bottle of lavender oil to keep around you so you can have that smell any time you want it. Your favourite things are important. They feed your soul and keep you grounded. Take some time to think about them and write them down. When I first did this exercise, I put my answers on little cards and laminated them to keep. I found over time that my favourite things changed as I discovered new favourite things, places, foods and fragrances.

Your values

What's important to you right now? Our values change over time. What we were passionate about as teenagers or young adults will not be the same as what we would fight for now. Understanding what your top five priorities are will help you make decisions about your life more easily. For example, if family holidays are a top priority, you may want to cut back on your spending in other areas so that you can afford to do this. Understanding what your values and priorities are also ties in with assertiveness. If you know what is important to you, it's easier to make decisions about how you want to live your life, and it will become easier to say 'no' to the things that don't align with your values.

How do you know when you are happy?

Similar to values and priorities, the things that make us happy change and shift over time. Taking a closer look at what makes you happy right now might be an eye-opener. My friend Thomas used to love working in sales. He loved the competition and the drive to win. Now, 11 years and two children later, he is happiest spending time at home. It doesn't always take a lavish holiday or a big adventure to be happy. Sometimes it's the simplest things, like growing vegetables on an allotment, a DIY project done well or having coffee with a friend. Happiness and contentment go hand in hand; if you have one, the other is not far away. As the parent of an autistic child, contentment is something you should make it your mission to seek out.

Feeling safe

What makes you feel safe? If something upsetting has happened, how do you help yourself recover? Knowing what makes you feel safe is very important. Parenting is full of scary and upsetting moments, close calls and things that make you angry. Having autism in the mix increases the likelihood of these kinds of things. Working out what will help you recover from stressful situations will assist you in doing so more quickly.

When I first looked at this for myself, I realized that feeling full (as in not hungry) and warm were key to my feeling safe. Because of this, I always keep tins of tomato soup on hand. I have a weighted blanket that is calming. I also have different music playlists on my phone that I listen to, depending on the situation. I have favourite, funny videos on YouTube bookmarked for easy access. Maybe for you, cuddling your dog makes you feel safe. Perhaps it's talking to your partner or a friend, or reading a favourite book or poem. Meditation or prayer may help you. Take some time to think about what these things are so that you can create your own emotional first aid kit.

Gratitude

There is a lot of talk about gratitude these days, so much that it's easy to gloss over the word when you see it in a magazine or on social media. Gratitude is crucially important for parents of autistic children, and so it is something to pay close attention to. Living a 'glass always half empty' life is not conducive to happiness.

When you first begin this journey, you focus on all of the things you don't have or can't do, and/or what your child can't manage. In fact, you may find yourself wallowing in a pit of self-pity and lack. The thing is that life – every life – is full of wonderful things to be grateful for. I am grateful for my toilet, hot water and having clothes to wear and food to eat. I'm grateful for the nights when my daughter sleeps, so that I can, too. When you begin to practise gratitude, you will shift your mindset from scarcity to abundance. Paying attention to what you have instead of focusing on what's missing is very powerful. It will make you feel rich!

Similar to gratitude is something I call 'golden moments'. Learn to look for the golden moments in life and not just the negative things that happen. I actively look for the golden moments in every day. Examples of recent golden moments include my daughter playing a game with me that made her laugh like a drain, her playing a song beautifully on the piano and tasting the first tomatoes grown in our garden. Just little things. I find if I focus on these things and not on the negative stuff, I feel happier and more in control of life. I've also noticed that I'm now actively seeking out the golden moments, not just trying to think about them at the end of the day.

Journaling

Writing can be a very powerful tool for managing stress and solving problems. I write almost every day. I aim to do this with my morning coffee. I don't have any goal or number of pages I need to fill. I just write about whatever is on my mind. I write as though I am writing a letter, explaining things that happened and how I feel about them. I write about sticky situations and what I think I should do. I write about my worries, but also my goals and dreams. Any time I am stressed, I write it out: what happened, why I am upset and what I might be able to do about the situation. Sometimes I don't have the answers about what action to take, but the writing still helps me to feel better and focus on potential solutions.

It may be difficult for you to write longhand because of a concern about privacy. If this is the case, try using a notes app on your phone where you can type out what's on your mind. I find that I never go back and read anything I write; it's the act of writing itself that does the job. It may be that you can type out everything and then just delete it. It's a bit like writing a letter to someone who you are angry at but then tearing it up and not sending it. The act of putting words on paper or screen really works.

The other option is to record voice messages. You can do this via a recording app on your phone. Find some time alone (if that is at all possible) and just record your thoughts as though you are having a conversation with a friend. Every week, my friend Sara and

I leave each other long, rambling voice messages. We both just talk in a freestyle way, sharing what is happening that day and what is generally going on in our lives. We both find it very therapeutic to do this, and so recording your thoughts may have the same effect for you.

Your dreams

Another part of self-care and not losing yourself in your child is holding on to your dreams, or even just working out what they are. Parenthood often makes a person re-evaluate what is important. Having a child out of school, lack of good, quality sleep and poor mental health can have an impact on your ability to work. I know several parents who have left work to look after their children. It can be difficult to find your way back to your chosen career after a break of a year or more. Whether or not this is what has happened in your life, it's important to work out what you want in your future. It's OK if working isn't your bag, but if you want or need to work, what is it that you really want to do?

I worked in marketing from my early twenties to my early forties. This was a career I fell into after I left university. While I did gain some skills and learned some new things, this period of my life mostly taught me that I don't like working for anyone else. I am a truly terrible employee. Instead of carrying on down this path, I began to work for myself. For many years I was a self-employed PA to creative people. I had interesting clients: a comedian, an art dealer, artists and some authors. Now I am focused on writing and training. I love the work I do. In fact, it doesn't feel like work at all.

What could you do with your life? If you have a job, do you love it? If not, is there a side hustle you could set up? The pandemic brought about a massive increase in the number of online 'sidepreneur' courses that teach people how to make money using the internet. Maybe there's an opportunity for you to do something different.

Perhaps you've always worked in an office but dream of being an artist, a hairdresser, a massage therapist or a driving instructor. Is there a way for you to pursue your dream alongside your current job?

Maybe your dream doesn't involve work, but volunteering with a cause close to your heart. Volunteering is wonderful. I have volunteered all of my adult life. Through volunteering, you can gain new skills you wouldn't in your current job and meet new people you wouldn't otherwise meet. Most importantly, it feels great to help people, and to feel you are making a difference in the world.

The best way to work out what you would like to do is to set time aside to write out all of the potential job ideas. Don't just list safe options, but include the risky ones, too. Once you have your long list, have a read through and notice which ones make you feel excited. These are the ones to pursue further.

Autism isn't stressful

Just as autism isn't scary or sad, neither is it stressful. Struggling to get support for your child in school is stressful. Lack of sleep is stressful. The unpredictability of your child's behaviour is stressful. Autism, in itself, is not stressful.

As a parent of an autistic child, you will have more stress than the average person, simply because there is so much more to worry about, learn about and manage. It's important that you take stress management very seriously; it is vital to your mental health and your ability to cope with all this life throws at you.

When my daughter was tiny, I read something that said that the stress of being the parent of an autistic child was similar to that of a combat soldier. I was offended when I read this. I didn't like the implication that autistic children were causing this level of stress. To be honest, at the time I read this, I didn't have much stress so this also had a bearing on my opinion.

It's easy to confuse our feelings about autism and our child with the difficulties that come with autism. It's important to be very clear in yourself that there is a distinct line between 'autism' and 'mucky stuff that comes along with autism'. And to be clear that your child is your child and that autism is part of who they are, but not everything that they are.

Stress is sneaky

Stress crept up on me over the years. For a long time, my daughter had a place in a school that I believed was good. She was generally calm and happy. Her sleep (and thus mine) was consistently good. Around the time the Covid pandemic began in early 2020, the wheels had started to come off with the school. I removed my daughter from the school, and this began a long period of her being out of full-time education, which is still going on as I write this.

The lack of routine caused by various lockdowns and my daughter being out of school created stress for us both. Her sleep and behaviour became erratic and unpredictable as she was distressed and unsettled much of the time. As her needs are high and complex, finding a new school was difficult. I was unable to work as much as I needed to due to the lack of childcare. All very stressful things.

I have met thousands of parents of autistic children over the past 11 years. Ninety-five per cent of them have been mothers who are carrying most of the load of supporting their child or children. Most of them have been stressed out by a great number of things, for example:

- the child's school refuses to support the child

- the child's other parent does not believe the child is autistic

- the parent has had to leave their job or is worried about being fired due to work absence

- the child refuses to go to school because the school is not supporting them appropriately

- money worries

- relationship issues

- difficulty in supporting more than one autistic child where the needs of the children are very different.

The number of parents I have met who have autoimmune conditions such as rheumatoid arthritis and fibromyalgia is shocking. There is a huge proportion of parents in our community who are depressed and suffer from anxiety. I have also met several parents who have MS and some who have Functional Neurological Disorder, debilitating neurological conditions thought to be caused by stress.

I don't share this to scare you but to press upon you that stress is a big deal. You will need to find ways to manage your stress levels. If stress is left unchecked, what happens is that the trigger mechanism for it becomes hypersensitive. Where once it took something big to cause stress, now the stress response is on a hair trigger, so you feel a lot more stressed a lot more of the time.

Strategies for reducing stress
Eat well

I mentioned this before, but it bears repeating. The better your diet is, the less stressed you will feel. If you can avoid eating processed foods and reduce your salt and sugar intake, you will feel better.

After trying several different ways of eating to reduce stress, I have found that a 'paleo' diet has the greatest impact on reducing stress for me. I mainly eat organic fresh fruit, vegetables, nuts, seeds and grass-fed meat. Although I am on a limited budget, eating well and the positive effect this has had on my health have made it worth my while to buy organic foods, which I often find in the reduced section of my supermarket. I recently cut out caffeine and this has reduced my stress and had a dramatic impact on the quality of my sleep.

Meditation

Meditation is also helpful for calming an anxious mind. There is no one right way to meditate. Some people clear their mind for a certain amount of time while others use the time to let ideas come to the surface. There are a lot of different meditations you can access for free online and some great meditation apps as well.

I am not good at meditation. My ADHD brain simply won't shut off and I spend the time thinking of a thousand things; I cannot quiet my mind despite putting a lot of effort into this. What does work for me, however, is guided meditation. This is when you listen to someone who guides you through going into a deep relaxed state, then through a mental journey, such as walking along a beach or through a forest, then brings you back out again. I can focus on this kind of meditation and I find it deeply relaxing.

Mindfulness

The practice of mindfulness is especially helpful for parents of children with additional needs. Mindfulness helps us to get off the worry-go-round by grounding us in the present moment. When you find yourself in a panic, stop and look around you. What can you see and hear? What is around you that you can touch? Is there a fragrance or scent in the air? A few minutes of bringing yourself back into the here and now can really help.

Although I am not good at meditation, I have come to love practising mindfulness. When I am stressed, I stop and look around at what I can see, hear, feel, smell and taste. Another tactic I use when I find my mind spinning on the past or future is to remind myself that whatever I'm worrying about is not happening right now, and this helps me to let the thoughts go. These strategies stop me worrying about the future or obsessing about the past.

Another thing I do is remind myself of the fact that I am safe and sound and have everything I need. I am blessed to live in a nice flat in a quiet place. It's good to remind ourselves of what we have instead of focusing on what we don't.

EFT

Another useful technique for quickly reducing stress and staying in the moment is something called Emotional Freedom Technique (EFT). EFT works by tapping on various points of your body to manage stress and shift emotional energy. It sounds strange and feels a bit odd when you first do it, but it really does work. When you do EFT, you use a script to guide you through the process. There are a lot of scripts online for this, just search for what you need, for example, 'EFT insomnia script'.

Breathing exercises

Breathing exercises are the quickest way to calm the nervous system. They can be done anytime and anywhere, are free and work immediately. I use breathing exercises several times a day to keep anxiety at bay. Generally, this involves simply taking a deep belly breath to the count of four, holding it for a count of five and breathing out to a count of eight. Or I will take a deep breath in and then take additional 'sips' of air in until I feel I can't take any more. I'll hold that breath, then let it go in a big exhale.

Focus on the positive

Last year my daughter went through a period when she was very distressed. At the end of every day I would tell my partner all of the bad things that had happened and how stressed I was. I became depressed and anxious, feeling we would never come out of the other side of this phase.

I decided that instead of focusing on the negative things that were happening, I would pay close attention to the positive things instead (these are the 'golden moments' I mentioned earlier). I stopped talking about the bad times. I began to see that even on the worst day, something beautiful happened. For example, one day she had a massive tantrum in the street that was scary and dangerous, but on the way home she sang in the car. I chose to hold on to the sound of her sweet voice singing and not the upset of the tantrum.

I got into the habit of doing this every day and it's made a huge difference to my mental health and ability to cope. I am better able to support my daughter through difficult times by reminding myself how wonderful she is every day.

It's been over a year since I changed my mindset. I have been amazed at how well this strategy has worked. Not only does it help me keep a positive outlook, but the challenging times are far less upsetting.

The fact is that when we focus on the negative things, we create a doom spiral for ourselves to spin around in. Negativity breeds negativity, and it's very important to push back against it and break this bad habit.

AUTISM AND RELATIONSHIPS – TIPS FOR SUCCESS

I've put this in the self-care section because if your relationship with your partner is solid, you both will have a far easier time weathering the storms of raising an autistic child. Here are some thoughts that another mother and I put together based on our own experiences.

Communication is key

- *Talk about your fears.* Openly discussing what you are both worried about brings things out into the open so that you can work on them together.

- *Have a debrief after challenging situations.* Talk to each other about what went wrong and what you will do differently in future. Remember that you both will feel upset or embarrassed or that you have failed during these times.

- *Keep in touch.* Have a rule that whoever is looking after the child/ren must text the other with updates about how things are going. Give your partner a heads up if something difficult has happened so they know what they are coming home to.

- *Form a tight team.* Decide that what you both believe is right for your family is right and do not let outside influences impact on your decisions.

- *Share the load.* It's easy for childcare responsibilities to fall mainly to one partner. However, it is very important that you share these responsibilities. Looking after your child is the best way to learn how to look after your child.

- *Make time for each other.* If possible, ask family or friends to help with childcare so that you can spend time alone together. If that's not an option, schedule dates during the school day.

- *Hang on to intimacy.* Don't turn away from each other out of fear – physical intimacy is a great calmer.

- *Tag team during challenging situations.* Sharing responsibility is especially important during challenging times. You must work together in order to keep everyone safe.

- *Look after your health.* Eat well and look after yourselves so that you have the energy to interact with each other.

- *Get help if you can't see eye to eye.* A third party in the form of a relationship counsellor or therapist can make all the difference.

Take a break

As a single mother, I am painfully aware of how difficult it is for some parents to take a break from their children. I know that this may be impossible for you right now. If there is a way for you to take a break, you need to do this. Time away from your child is restorative and will help you keep hold of your self.

Talking therapies

Depending on your area, there may be talking therapies available to you on the NHS, or you may want to seek out a private counsellor who can help you talk through your stressors. In my experience, the therapist or counsellor does not need to have any experience of autism. A good therapist can help you work through whatever is happening for you.

Exercise

It bears repeating: moving your body in any way will reduce stress. Using big muscles in your arms, legs and trunk is very effective for calming your nervous system. I know that formal exercise isn't for everyone, and sometimes our child's needs don't allow us to do this. Hoovering, simple stretches and dancing are all great ways to get moving. The more exercise you get, the better you will feel.

A note about medication

If you are very depressed and/or anxious, you may want to speak to your doctor about trying medication. Please do your research before trying this option as medication is not a quick fix and can have unpleasant side effects. I took Prozac for depression for about five years. When some things in my life shifted, I decided to stop taking it. Shortly thereafter, something upset me and I cried. I realized that I had not cried in the entire time I'd been on medication – five years! – and that all of my other emotions had been dulled as well, including happiness. I feel that Prozac also impacted on my capacity to make decisions. The choice is yours; make it wisely.

You may find that making small life changes, like swapping coffee for camomile tea (it was tough but I did it, and you can, too) or using over-the-counter calming herbal remedies may do the job. Nutrition and supplements have always been a special interest of mine. I spend a lot of time researching different options for improving cognition and reducing anxiety. For a variety of reasons, I don't take medication for ADHD, so I like to take different supplements to boost my brain power, such as L-Tyrosine and Co-Q10. For anxiety, I take calcium and magnesium. I also regularly take valerian tablets.

I've shared all of this with you to remind you that you are important and worthy of looking after. The ways you can look after yourself are simple and inexpensive. It's not an option to skip self-care. I've put more extensive information about self-care options for you at wdisbook.com/resources.

CHAPTER 7

Are You Autistic?

It would be remiss of me not to include information to guide you through what to do if, through the process of getting your child assessed and diagnosed, you begin to think that you are or may be autistic. You are not alone in this realization; this experience is extremely common in our community.

Until fairly recently, autism was believed to be a severe condition with obvious visible traits. If you are over the age of about 40, this would have been true when you were a child. Your behaviours and social difficulties would have simply been thought of as quirkiness or shyness. Our parents simply didn't know what we know now. I believe this is especially true for those of us who grew up in small towns or villages, where, in those pre-internet days, information from the wider world wasn't always available.

The realization that you may be autistic may shock you. It might make you question a lot of things about your life, including your current life situation, job, relationship, and so on. This is extremely unsettling. If you are going through this, be very careful with your-self. Don't make any snap decisions (I know this is hard, given the black and white way we think). Just let the process unfold.

The first thing to do if you believe you may be autistic is to see your GP. He or she will ask you questions about why you feel this way. You may need to justify your views, which is annoying but part of the process. They will then refer you on to the assessment team in your area. Depending on where you live, there could be a long wait for assessment.

Private assessment for adults is also available. It is expensive, but if you are able to afford it, it is often far quicker.

Sometimes, a person just wants a diagnosis for themselves. A diagnosis is validation and also justification. An autism diagnosis can be like discovering a missing part of your identity. We can share it with those around us to explain why we are struggling and why we do the things we do.

The Equality Act 2010 defines disability as a physical or mental impairment that has a significant effect on a person's life over a long period of time. The Act does not specify that a disability must have a formal diagnosis in order to be recognized. This means that if you are struggling at work or in school, you should get help with the things you are struggling with. However, it is fair to say that having a formal diagnosis will ease this process.

I found learning that I was autistic both wonderful and heart-breaking. I explain this in far more detail in the next chapter. It was great to finally understand why everything was so hard, and why I felt so out of place all of the time. However, I could see the damage that I had done to others through thoughtless acts and words, and that I could never go back and fix anything. I also realized I didn't have a clue who I was or what I wanted in life. I'm pleased to say I've fully recovered from the upset of looking back at the past and now have a happy, fulfilling and productive life.

The other thing that may happen for you during the process of getting your child assessed is that you realize your partner is autistic. Please understand that they may not be receptive to hearing this information. Be patient with it as it is a lot to take on, and it's much better for a person to come to understand this themselves, in their own way and in their own time. Telling a person you think they are autistic because they do this or that might actually be quite offensive to that person. Tread carefully; a compassionate approach is needed.

You may find it helpful to read books about understanding autism in relationships so that you can better get to grips with why your partner does the things they do. These will help you to see your part in the relationship and to feel less upset about things your partner does that may look cold or careless from the outside. I have had autistic partners and have found it useful to look at something called *Love Languages,*[1] which explains that each of us has different ways of expressing love.

Although it can be disquieting to realise that you are autistic, once you get your head around it, your life may change for the better as things start making sense. A lot of the information in this book about self-care and how to help your child will help you with this process. I've put some useful links and other information about this at wdisbook.com/resources.

---

1   Chapman, G. (2015). *Love Languages: The Secret to Love That Lasts.* Moody Publishers.

PART 2

How to Help Your Child

This book is a guide to managing the emotional aspects of raising an autistic child. It may seem strange therefore to have a great portion dedicated to helping your child. What I know is that there is a parent–child happiness continuum; happy children make happy parents and vice versa. I must tell you how you can best support your child as this will improve life for both of you.

Every autistic person is very different to every other autistic person. Autism is a complicated, often mysterious condition. As such, when you first begin seeking out ways to best support your child, you may become overwhelmed very quickly.

This section covers what I feel are the main issues you will need to address to best support your child. I'll cover the 'big five' key areas your child needs help in, some general, but vital information, how to talk about autism and getting education support for your child. This will set you up on a solid path for making a big difference in your child's life.

CHAPTER 8

To Diagnose or Not to Diagnose

However pronounced your child's differences are, one thing is certain: you will doubt your decision to seek a diagnosis many, many times while you wait for the assessment to take place. Even if your child is quite affected by autism, some variation of 'they seem fine this week, maybe I am wrong', will undoubtedly cross your mind. This is entirely normal. Nobody chooses autism, and it's understandable to want to talk yourself out of it. However, I urge you to stick to your path; stay on the waiting list for assessment and diagnosis.

Some parents struggle with the decision to go for a diagnosis for their child. This may be down to pressure put on them by the people in their support network. Well-meaning friends and family members may say things like 'why do you want to label her?' or 'if he gets diagnosed, he won't be able to join the military', which might make it difficult for you to choose to have your child assessed.

While the internet can be beneficial for parents of autistic children, it can also be a fear-mongering bully. Misinformation about autism is rife. The message that 'children grow out of autism' understandably creates indecision and worry that seeking a diagnosis for your child is a bad idea. If your parental gut feeling is telling you that your child may be autistic, it is crucial that you follow that hunch as it's most likely correct.

Why it's important to pursue a diagnosis for your child

An autism diagnosis is for life, not just for childhood, which may make you worry whether or not you should seek this for your child. The best way I can explain why a diagnosis is so important is to tell you my story.

Shortly after my daughter was diagnosed with autism in 2012, I stumbled upon Samantha Craft's 'unofficial list' (actually a set of lists) of autism traits in women (see link at wdisbook.com/resources). Reading through the lists, I felt like Samantha had been watching me in my own life and taking notes. It was almost eerie to read through these characteristics as so many of them fit me: deep thinker, honest, naïve, difficulty making friends, likes to be alone, and so on.

I dived into researching autism in women, and it quickly became apparent that I was very likely autistic. This was a painful realization. The information about autism in women and girls made so much sense but also shone a light on all of the negative ways it had impacted on my entire life. I felt as though I was standing at the top of a mountain, looking down over 40+ years of failed relationships, jobs and friendships, not to mention all of the stupid, insensitive things I had said and done in all those years. I desperately wanted the mountain to open up and swallow me whole.

I got a referral for an assessment by our local autistic adult team. I had to write a letter to the team justifying why I believed I was autistic and how I felt a diagnosis would improve my life. It must have been convincing as the referral was successful.

At the time of the appointment, I was in a good place, mental health-wise. I was excited to meet the team, given that I was also an autism professional and was interested in how the assessment would be carried out.

I was meant to have my family members fill out forms to describe what I was like as a child. I knew that asking my elderly parents and older sister to do this would make them uncomfortable, and I believed they would not have supported my decision to seek a diagnosis. I had my partner complete the forms instead, giving the clearest picture he could of what I had been like over our years together.

During the assessment, I was friendly and chatty. I talked about how autism had affected me and my life over the years. I talked about my current work with the autism support charity. I was positive and upbeat.

I didn't get a diagnosis.

Apparently, I was 'too sociable' and 'too self-aware' to be autistic. Now that I am many years down the line from this experience, I can see that I masked my way through the assessment. It was an unfamiliar situation for me, so I put on a cheerful, business-like persona to get through it.

Being denied a diagnosis was so frustrating. I had been in quite a dark place with my mental health just months before. I believe that if I had had the assessment during that time, I would have been given a diagnosis as it would have been clearer how, at times, autism negatively impacts my life.

The lack of diagnosis made me feel like a fraud. I knew that I was autistic, but without the official seal of approval, I didn't feel like I could claim it. I struggled for a few years with this before realizing that self-identification within the autistic adult community is an acceptable option. This is the route I have taken. I now proudly identify as autistic.

It would never have occurred to my parents that I was autistic when I was a child in the 1970s and 80s. Society's view of autism was entirely different then, and my autistic traits at the time would have been wholly overlooked. I was a shy, socially awkward, insular child. Our household was chaotic when I was growing up, and I easily flew under the radar by being the 'good girl' and not making a fuss. I learned from a very young age that it was best to hide my true feelings and mask my way through family life which was turbulent at best. There would have been nothing especially obvious to my family to indicate that I was struggling in a world that, to me, was very confusing.

Fortunately, I found schoolwork easy (but boring) and successfully made it through school. I went on to a university that was far from home, and it was here that the cracks began to appear. At secondary school, I had a small circle of friends, but at university, my inability to fit in was agonizing. I became very depressed, but didn't realize I was depressed as there was no one around me to point it out. I was a fine art major but lost the ability to be creative and produce art. I changed majors to journalism, but this only made things worse as it required a lot of interaction with people, which was impossible for me.

At the time, I was involved in a long-distance relationship with a musician. I did not want to move back home but could not cope with university, so I made the ill-advised decision to move in with him. We subsequently married, and I fell into working in marketing. The marriage failed, and so did the first job and the second job. Thus began a long, painful cycle of marriages and divorces, starting and leaving jobs.

From my 20s into my 40s, I was a champion masker. I would meet a man and become everything he needed me to be. I'd shape-shift into the perfect partner; I'd take on his interests and hobbies and cook and eat the food he liked. After six months or two years or five years, this became utterly untenable. I could no longer manage the bowling, sci-fi, boozy nights out, or whatever it was I'd taken on as the perfect chameleon companion, and the whole thing would unravel like the inside of a golf ball.

I carried out a similar but less emotionally damaging act at work. I loved job seeking and saw it as a fun game. Although I had excellent skills and experience, I still felt the need to morph into the perfect employee. For a few months, I'd be the life and soul of the company. I once even won a 'best newcomer' award for my company spirit. However, it was all an act as I didn't know how people behaved socially, and it was never long before my co-workers realized I was just a bit... odd.

Another work difficulty was that I could always clearly see what was wrong within each company and set about to fix it, even when I wasn't asked to do this. While some employers embraced my enthusiasm, most just saw me as a pain in the backside, and it could make for a very awkward work atmosphere. I simply didn't get that I was just a cog in the machine. My propensity to voice unsolicited ideas above my station was legendary.

Things slowly began to change once I realized I was autistic. Because I had spent all my adult life unintentionally pretending to be someone else, I woke up in my early 40s to realize I had no idea who I was. What do *I* like? What do *I* want to do? I did a lot of work around learning what my favourite things are and what makes me feel safe.

I was blessed to be part of an autism charity, which meant I was naturally surrounded by other neurodivergent people or those who were pro-autism and thus accepting of me and my quirks. I learned that working for others, especially in a Monday–Friday, nine-to-five office environment, was a poison chalice for me. Over the past 11 years, I have been able to design a life for myself that takes into account my own special needs for the right sensory environment, organization and movement breaks.

I no longer have to mask my way into romantic relationships or friendships. I'm just myself, and a lot of people seem to like this straight-up version of me.

This was a long-winded way for me to say to you: pursue the diagnosis. An autism diagnosis is not just about getting support in school (and shouldn't be anyway, because the law states that a child must be supported whether or not they have a diagnosed condition). It's about your child's identity, not just now but for life. It's about helping them find their place in the world and helping them to unmask and just be themselves. It's about teaching them self-advocacy based on their understanding of how autism affects them. It's about keeping them safe from harm because they understand their social strengths and weaknesses, which will enable them to ask for help when it's needed.

It's important to remember that whether or not you pursue an assessment, your child is neurodivergent. You owe it to them to seek a diagnosis so they will not go through life as I did. I spent all my adult life up to my early 40s lost and confused about why life was so hard. Again, I don't blame my parents. Still, if I had been diagnosed as a child or teenager, life would have made so much more sense, and I wouldn't have spent decades feeling like a desperately struggling fish out of water.

Give your child the gift of a diagnosis and the subsequent knowledge and understanding that will follow on from this.

Private autism assessments

In the UK, the waiting list for NHS autism assessment is long. In some areas the wait is over two years. This long delay creates a lot of problems. If you feel your child will not cope in mainstream school, they will need to have a diagnosis in order to go to an autism specialist provision, but you may not get a diagnosis before they start school. Although the law states that a child's need for support in school is not diagnosis-dependent, there are unfortunately many schools who don't understand this and so your child may go without vital support while they are awaiting diagnosis and assessment.

If you are financially able, you may choose to have a private assessment instead. The cost for a private assessment is, at the time of writing, between £1500 and £3000. It's important to note that whether done privately or on the NHS, there is no guarantee that a diagnosis will be given. If you choose to go privately, the practitioner must assess your child with at least one other practitioner and the assessment must be based on NICE (National Institute for Health and Care Excellence) guidelines.

Even if the practitioner you choose provides the gold standard of assessment service, your local authority and NHS are not obligated to accept the diagnosis. It is advised that you also go through the NHS assessment and diagnosis process to ensure that your child's diagnosis is officially documented and recognized. In my experience, every situation is different. I know many people who have had a private diagnosis accepted by their local authority and some people who have not. It's worth speaking to the school, the local diagnosing team and the local authority's SEND team to determine what they require in order to accept a private diagnosis.

Is there an autism epidemic?

The rates of autism diagnosis have increased dramatically over the past 20 years. From 1998 to 2018, there was a 787 per cent increase in autism diagnoses across all ages including adults.[1] At first glance this may be alarming. What could be causing this massive increase in autism diagnoses? The fact is that there is not an increase in autism itself, but in the recognition and awareness of the condition.

If you are over the age of 40, think of how people talked about autism when you were a child. Chances are that there was very little discussion about the condition. Unless a person also had an obvious learning difficulty or disability, an autistic person likely went undiagnosed simply because he was not obviously autistic. While today we know that autistic people don't look any different to non-autistic people, this only became mainstream knowledge in the 2000s.

Consider how many television shows, films, books, plays and even children's cartoons now have an autistic character. This would have been rare before the 1990s. While *Rainman* came out in 1988 and *What's Eating Gilbert Grape* in 1991, these films were very unusual in their inclusion of an autistic main character. These days we have a wealth of great autistic leads such as Sam in Atypical, Saga in The Bridge and the Extraordinary Attorney Woo.

While society still has a long way to go in terms of awareness and acceptance of autism, great strides have been made. This is great news for our children and for us as well. I don't think I've spoken to a single person about autism in the past 11 years who didn't have some autism connection. Mention it to the person in the queue at the supermarket and she'll say, 'oh, my nephew/neighbour/cousin is autistic'. Let this be a comfort to you. You are far from alone on this journey.

---

[1]   Russell, G., Stapley, S., Newlove-Delgado, T., Salmon, A., White, R., Warren, F., Pearson, A. & Ford, T. (2021). Time trends in autism diagnosis over 20 years: a UK population-based cohort study. *Journal of Child Psychology and Psychiatry*, 63(6), 674–682. https://doi.org/10.1111/jcpp.13505

CHAPTER 9

The Dark Secret

As parents (and humans), we all want to be in control. We need to feel capable and that we can look after and help our children, no matter what happens. If a problem arises, we can sort it out. If an injury occurs, we can soothe it. We are compelled to eradicate whatever gets in the way of our child's happiness and wellbeing.

Autism doesn't care about any of this. When autism first enters your life, you will suddenly feel out of control. When we feel like we are losing control, we do whatever we can to get it back.

When I first realized my daughter is autistic, we saw our local GP, and he referred my daughter to the community paediatrician. After observing her and asking us some questions, the paediatrician said, very casually, with a slight shrug, 'it might be autism'. He said this with no gravity, like a person might say, 'I'm off to lunch'.

I left the appointment thinking, 'OK, so it might be autism, but that's clearly no big deal. I don't like the idea of autism, so I won't be having any of that, thank you very much! Not on my watch.'

We were at that time living in a rural county where autism was not diagnosed until the age of seven. Every few months, we'd have an appointment with the paediatrician who still said, 'it might be autism', but offered no advice or support for how we could help our child for the next five years until she'd be eligible for assessment.

I was at home with my two-year-old nonspeaking daughter all day, every day. I was totally isolated. I had no friends or family locally, and I had no support. As my daughter became more insular and disconnected from me, I became more frightened of what would happen to her.

I felt completely out of control, so I did what every single parent of a child suspected to be autistic does: I turned to the internet. I knew nothing about autism besides the negative connotations presented by the media, films and books. I'm not proud to admit that in my ignorance, the first thing I searched for was 'autism cure', and down the rabbit hole I went.

In my naïve quest to carry out Operation Autism Elimination, I fed my daughter supplements, put her on a gluten-free and casein-free (GF/CF) diet and gave her clay and Epsom salt baths. I read the GAPS book (which you will probably stumble across yourself on your autism journey). I made bone broth and strange pancakes from coconut flour and eggs.

When my daughter was two-and-a-half, I returned to work and put her with a childminder who also looked after other children. I faced the fact that it was impossible to insist she only feed my child GF/CF foods. I had to come to terms with how my daughter might not only eat bread but – gasp! – spaghetti hoops from a tin!

I prepared myself for a significant change in my child once she started going to this childminder. I thought that if her behaviour changed or she became more distant, I would put her straight back on the diet. What happened after she stopped the GF/CF protocol? Nothing. Well, not nothing – she put on weight. She got some colour back into her cheeks. She became healthier. To add insult to injury, before the diet, my daughter had eaten a wide variety of foods. After the diet, she stuck firmly to a beige food diet (porridge, toast, pasta, rice cakes). This has not changed over the past 11 years. Painful lesson learned.

Like most parents, I didn't talk to anyone about what I was doing to 'cure' autism. I felt that I'd done dozens of hours of research and that this made me a capable practitioner. I believed that I was doing the best things for my daughter. Looking back on this time, I can see that all I wanted was to feel in control, and I did for a while. For this reason, I didn't tell anyone what I was doing because I didn't want anyone to tell me to stop.

This chapter is called 'The Dark Secret' because so many of us do this. We try all of this alternative stuff but keep it to ourselves.

We turn our children into guinea pigs when we need to regain command of the situation. We try different 'tools' recommended by the internet:[1] restrictive diets, homeopathy, acupuncture, cranial osteopathy, special baths, grounding sheets, biofeedback and aromatherapy, just to name a few. These things are in the expensive but relatively harmless section of the autism cure supermarket.

In the expensive and extremely dangerous department are things like Miracle Mineral Solution (MMS), which is essentially bleach, that parents are told to give their children to eliminate the 'autism-causing toxins'. Other products and procedures recommended to parents include chelation therapy (again said to remove toxins), faecal implantation and shock treatment. These recommendations are dangerous and potentially deadly.

Autism is a genetic condition. Vaccines and mercury-based dental fillings do not cause it. It is not caused by electromagnetic fields, glyphosate or gluten. It is hereditary, and chances are you may see it in yourself and several family members. I am well aware that fierce arguments abound on this topic. However, I feel the facts are with genetics and the well-documented experiences of autistic adults that attest to autism running along family lines for generations.

The GF/CF diet is one of the most prolifically recommended 'treatments' for autism. Bowel issues such as diarrhoea and constipation are indeed relatively common among autistic children. If your child is suffering from digestive problems, keep a journal of what they eat and how they feel and act. After a few weeks, take your child to a doctor and discuss your observations. Let the doctor give you advice on what to do.

Arbitrarily putting your child on a restrictive diet with no medical basis is a bad idea. Doing this may cause them to develop sensitivities and other issues not present before you put them on the diet. Additionally, buying gluten- and casein-free foods is expensive.

---

[1]   To be clear, all of these treatments have their place in helping to relieve an individual's distress or discomfort and to improve their wellbeing. Here I am only referring to alternative therapies in the context where they are used to 'cure' autism. Additionally, some of these are invasive treatments that may be best left until a child is of an age where they can choose whether or not they want to take part.

I know from experience that feeling out of control is very uncomfortable. Autism can make us feel out of control as it's not something we can fix or cure. Your child needs love and acceptance of who they are: a beautiful, perfect, autistic being. It can be quite a journey moving from fear to acceptance, but you must do this to support your child and provide them with opportunities for happiness and success.

CHAPTER 10

How to Advocate for Your Child

Who do we need to talk to?

Your child has many people around them – at school, friends, siblings, at church, relatives, and so on. Some are more peripheral, like neighbours, distant relatives and work colleagues. Who you talk to, when you talk to them and what you tell people depends entirely on your life situation. For example, you may not need to say anything about your child to work colleagues, but if, for example, your child has school anxiety or is not attending for some other reason, you may need to speak to your employer to work out a more flexible way of working.

You will need to talk about your child's difficulties with people who are in a position to help them and/or you. Staff at school need to understand your child's needs so that they can provide appropriate support. The people closest to you, your friends and family, need to know so that they can provide practical help. The optician, dentist and hairdresser may need to know about your child's needs in order to best support them in their respective professional capacities.

You do not need to explain your child's behaviour, needs, difficulties or anything else to random strangers, neighbours or the general public. If you feel a need to do this, check in with yourself as to why this is. For example, if your child has a meltdown in a supermarket, there is no need to explain to people who witness this that your child is autistic. Your child is a perfect autistic being. Autism needs no explanation or defence.

It can be very difficult to talk about the challenges your child faces. You must find a balance between giving helpful information and respecting your child's dignity. This can be difficult as at times you will need to share information that may be embarrassing to your son or daughter to get them the support they need. Also, you will share information about your child to make things easier for them but, equally, you won't want them to – and often they don't want to – appear different to their peers.

As you travel along on your autism journey, you'll learn what's important to share and what isn't necessary. If your child is more cognitively able, you may be able to discuss with them what you plan to say and how you will say it, so that they are more comfortable with what is happening.

What to tell people

For your child to be well supported, you need to share with the people closest to them information about anything that impacts on their ability to participate and/or learn. What sensory needs do they have? Is your child anxious? What medical issues do they have? What is their learning style, and how do they best assimilate information? Do they have any communication issues? These are all very important factors in how your child accesses activities and learning opportunities.

Below are some things to think about regarding the information you may need to tell people about your son or daughter.

Sensory differences

You may have such an intuitive understanding of your child's sensory needs that it's difficult to work out what to say about them. Just think of what they struggle with and how you avoid upset for them. I cover sensory issues in detail in Chapter 15, but here are some ideas on what you may need to share about your child in terms of sensory differences. In addition to the main five senses (sight, hearing, taste, touch and smell), there are others you need to look into, such as proprioception (the sense of where your body is in space), the vestibular sense (which controls balance) and interoception (understanding your body's signals such as hunger, thirst and the need to use the toilet).

Here are some ideas of the kinds of sensory differences you will need to tell people to help them support your child:

- *Sensitivity to noise:* needs ear defenders, low or no music, a quiet space to work.

- *Visual sensitivity:* may wear sunglasses or tinted lenses, need plain walls and a neutral environment at home and school.

- *Sensitivity to touch:* may not like being touched or hugged, may be sensitive to clothing (for example labels in clothing, school uniform, aprons, coveralls, etc.), may struggle with messy play, messy projects, and so on.

- *Taste sensitivity:* may eat a very limited range of foods, eat foods in a certain order or certain way, may not try new foods.

- *Smell sensitivity:* may need those around them to avoid perfumes, strong washing powder, may struggle with scents in general, for example food smells.

Anxiety

If your child suffers from anxiety, as most autistic individuals do, this may cause them distress. To reduce upset, you will need to explain this to people who care for your child. Share with them what makes your child anxious, for example: sensory issues, not understanding expectations, unclear instructions, changes in routine or transition from one thing to another. Explain how they can prevent distress by supporting your child's sensory needs, providing clear instructions, giving advance notice of changes in routine and transitions from one activity to another. You also need to tell them how to comfort your child if they become distressed, for example, provide a quiet space, let them leave the room, listen to music, or whatever else your child might require to calm down.

Learning style

Does your child listen better while they are doing something else? For example, are they more able to focus if they have a fidget toy or are listening to music or white noise? Some children with autism also have ADHD, which can impact learning in a big way. Your child may need regular breaks from their desk to clear their head and refocus. He or she may need sensory or movement breaks to burn off excess energy. They may need regular reminders of what to do next. As a parent, you are not often with your child in a learning environment, but you can use a bit of detective work and observation at home to determine these things. Start paying attention to your child when they are learning a new skill or task at home, as this will help you understand their needs so that you can explain them to others.

Communication difficulties

You may have a child who is nonspeaking and/or has other communication challenges. It is unfortunately very common for people to think that a nonspeaking child is not intelligent, or that they also have a hearing impairment. Even if a child is very verbal, they may still have difficulties expressing themselves, especially when upset.

For example, some children may muddle up facts when talking about something upsetting that has happened. This is not usually intentional but simply how their brain processes information and the child's ability to express themselves. The brain and mouth don't always work together! It's important to tell people looking after your child about their specific communication difficulties so that they can factor these in. You will need to clearly explain how your child communicates with others, how others can communicate with your child and if your child needs extra processing time to take in things that are said to them.

Discuss challenges and not diagnosis

Remember how you felt when you first began to realise that your child is autistic? You will likely have felt, as I did, that autism is a negative condition. Bear in mind that the people you speak to about your child's needs may also have this view of autism. Saying 'my son is autistic' may not be helpful, as the person you are speaking to may have little or no knowledge of autism, or they may have an unhelpful, stereotypical view of the condition. It is often better to talk about your child's needs instead of their diagnosis. For example:

- 'Sarah has difficulty following spoken instructions, please can you write things down for her?' (Or perhaps you can work with the professional to create simple visuals).

- 'Edward has food sensitivities, so we will send him with his own food.'

- 'Tilly has sensitivities to noise so may want to wear ear defenders.'

- 'Louie prefers to work alone.'

Sometimes we need to do the work

If you are dealing with someone who truly doesn't have a clue what you are talking about you will need to provide them with things to help your child. Visuals, snacks your child will eat, ear defenders, and so on. It can be frustrating to do this but be patient; you are helping them to help your child.

Unfriendly, unhelpful people are everywhere

We've all encountered judgemental, unpleasant people. It's important to understand that there is no way to change these people. If there is someone like this in a position of authority with your child, it's time to change. Find a new scout group, GP or football club. You may get overly caught up, for way too long, in worrying about upsetting these kinds of people. There may be a financial consideration; for example, you will lose money by taking your child out of a class or group. Remember that what is most important is the wellbeing of your child and act accordingly.

Avoid functioning labels

It's difficult not to fall into the habit of using what are called 'functioning labels': describing your child as either 'high functioning' or 'low functioning'. A child who is labelled as 'high functioning' may be academically able and highly verbal, but may also have difficulty with self-care such as using the toilet and washing themselves. A child may be described as 'low functioning' if they have difficulties with learning and poor communication skills, but they may have also taught themselves to play the piano and type 80 words per minute.

Using functioning labels fails to take into account the whole person – the whole garden, not just a few flowers. A person labelled as 'high functioning' will often have unreasonably lofty expectations placed on her. On the flip side, a person classed as 'low functioning' may be discounted and denied opportunities to develop and learn.

ABOUT 'PROFOUND AUTISM'

As I write, there is a lot of talk in the news and on social media about the term, 'profound autism'. There is a call to make this an official sub-group of autism. In the past, I would have agreed with this sentiment, and would have said that my daughter is profoundly autistic. However, what I now know is that what makes autism appear 'profound' in some individuals is, in fact, learning disability.

In the UK there is no set pathway for the assessment and diagnosis of learning disability (something I am working to change). Children are diagnosed with learning disability by lottery, it seems, with some getting a diagnosis and some not. My daughter is a 13-year-old girl who presents as a toddler, and I have been fighting for over a year to get a diagnosis of learning disability for her.

There are many problems with the lack of a set diagnostic pathway. First, it denies support from services like CAMHS learning disability teams as some require a diagnosis. Second, as parents, we are led to believe that whatever is happening with our child is all to do with autism. Learning disability and autism are very distinct and separate things. If a child cannot use a toilet independently,[1] this is not about autism but learning disability.

'Profound autism' is not a thing. If you feel that your child is profoundly autistic, I urge you to seek advice about learning disability. It may be that there is support and help available under this umbrella that is very different to what you may receive by just pursuing support for autism-related issues.

In my (painfully hard-won) experience, the best way to get the ball rolling with this is to ensure that your child has a cognitive assessment. This will be done through your local authority's educational psychology team. You need to do all you can to get learning disability documented as this will make a huge difference in your child's life, especially as they enter adulthood. For more information about this, see wdisbook.com/resources.

Similarly, the term 'mild autism' is not appropriate. There is no such thing as 'mild autism'. Saying someone has mild autism means the autism is experienced in a mild way by the people around that person. Autism is never 'mild' for the autistic person. I find the best descriptor is around care needs, for example, 'my daughter has high and complex care needs', meaning she needs help in all areas of her life. A child with 'low care needs' would be more able to look after themselves (dress themselves, use the toilet independently, make a sandwich, and so on).

In 2013, the Diagnostic and Statistical Manual of Mental Disorders, Fifth Edition (DSM-5), which provides international guidelines for the diagnosis of Autism Spectrum Disorder (ASD), dropped Asperger Syndrome as a diagnosis. Asperger Syndrome was also referred to as 'high functioning autism'. Now, all forms of ASD are under one large umbrella. This is either problematic or positive, depending on your perspective.

It is natural for a parent who is new to autism to want to understand

---

1   For example, needing help with pulling trousers down and up, wiping themselves, flushing, washing hands and not strictly sensory issues which would be to do with autism and sensory processing.

where on the spectrum their child falls, as though there is a linear scale. The process through which a parent comes to terms with autism may include this emotional weighing and measuring of their child's skills and deficits. Some parents would like to believe that their child is less autistic than another child.

Going back to my garden analogy, think of it this way: is one flower better than another? Is the small flower less beautiful than the tall flower? I don't mean to be simplistic here, but it is crucial to remember, as a parent and a human being, that all children are equally valuable, lovable and worthy of care.

Autism is a complex condition that impacts each person in very different ways. I would love for my daughter to be less anxious and have an easier time communicating her needs. However, I would never want to take her autism away. Autism has brought abundant gifts of great creativity, imagination, music and fun to our lives.

I understand that you may not feel the same way about your child's autism. If you are struggling to see autism in a positive light, start by paying attention to the wonderful things your child does and the helpful traits they have. This may help you shift your mindset.

'Has autism' or 'is autistic'?

Every parent of an autistic child desperately wants to help their child. They urgently want to solve all of the problems and fix all of the issues. At first, the parent will believe that autism is the problem, and that all of the issues stem from this. The trouble with this mindset is that autism is integral to the autistic person. It's no different than their eye colour or the sound of their voice.

Some people prefer to say, 'my child is autistic', and others say, 'my child has autism'. In my opinion there is no one right way to refer to your child. My advice is to use whichever feels right for you until your child is of an age when they can choose for themselves, and then respect their decision.

You may encounter people who will fiercely debate this issue. There is a lot of talk in online autism forums about 'person-first language', which states that the person is separate from the condition. Examples of person-first language would be 'my son has autism' or 'she is a person with autism'. Others will passionately argue that 'autistic person', 'I am autistic,' or 'my daughter is autistic' are the appropriate terms.

A great deal of energy can be wasted debating this point that would be far better spent in other, more productive ways. Whichever side of this argument you agree with, the most important thing to understand is that autism is a lifelong condition that is a part of your child. It cannot be separated from them, no matter how you choose to refer to it.

CHAPTER 11

Getting Started with Supporting Your Child

When I was running an autism charity, we received an endless stream of emails from parents who were new to autism and desperate to know how to help their child. I know that it can feel overwhelming and stressful at this point, when you feel like you don't know anything but also feel you need to sort everything out all at once. You feel helpless, worried and alone.

I want to help you get right to the heart of what will help your child. There are five main areas that every autistic child needs help with:

- executive functioning

- anxiety

- emotional regulation

- sensory differences

- communication.

Of course, throughout their life, they will need help with all sorts of things. However, these five are the biggies and the ones you must gain a solid understanding of in order to best help your child thrive. Focusing on these five things will also reduce your own anxiety and improve your confidence as a parent. The following chapter focuses on these, but before I get to them, I need to share some other information with you.

The myth of early intervention

When you first set out on your autism journey and are searching the internet for whatever it is you feel will help you at that time, there is one term you will see again and again: 'early intervention'. I have never found a solid definition for 'early intervention'. I am not talking about the sort of early intervention every child needs – socializing, care and comfort – but the autism-specific brand of early intervention that is touted by many (often American) websites. The idea seems to be that for an autistic child to have any sort of positive outcome, their caretakers must dive into hiring therapists and professionals to help them, from a very young age, with their speech, sensory and emotional regulation and – depending on the website – the aim may also be for the child to generally appear less autistic. See the previous page for information about ABA therapy.

There are significant flaws in this plan. Firstly, many parents don't realize their child is autistic until well beyond their toddler years. Secondly, most parents, even if they did realize that their child was autistic from a very early age, are not financially in a place to hire an army of therapists to support their child.

In my experience, parents of children who are well beyond the age of five read about early intervention, and it puts them into a state of absolute despair. They think they've missed the magic early intervention bus and that it is too late to help their child. They believe their child is doomed and that this is because they, the parent, have failed to do this early intervention stuff.

The great news is that early intervention is a myth. Of course, if when our children were 18–24 months old, all of us could have enlisted a team of people to help them in all the areas they required help with, this would have been great. But most of us didn't, couldn't or can't do that, and this is absolutely OK because of the magic of something called neuroplasticity.

Neuroplasticity is your friend

Until the mid-1960s, it was generally believed that our brains developed until around the age of 25 and then stopped growing and became fixed. Fortunately, scientists discovered that this is not true; our brains can grow and reorganize themselves throughout our lives.

If a person were to have a stroke that damaged the part of the brain that controlled speech, it is possible that the brain could reorganize itself so that speech is directed from a different, undamaged part of the brain. If you want to learn a new language or retrain for a new career, neuroplasticity makes it possible for you to do that.

For our children, neuroplasticity means they can learn new skills anytime. While it is true that young children's brains are more 'plastic' and malleable than those of older people, the fact remains that brains are more or less changeable for our entire lives. Your child can learn self-care and social and communication skills at any time. A nonspeaking child can begin to speak at any time. There is no cut-off point.

My daughter did not speak until the age of four-and-a-half. When she was around three, her grandparents took her out for a walk around our city centre. While they were out, they got to chatting to a well-meaning stranger who, upon realizing that my daughter wasn't speaking, told the grandparents, 'if she doesn't speak by the time she's four, she never will'. (They unfortunately believed this 'advice'.) This kind of information is so damaging, especially because it is utter nonsense. Children can learn and gain new skills at any time.

Resist overwhelm

Every autistic child is different and has different challenges and needs. Learning that your child may be or is autistic puts you on an intense learning curve. I say it is like climbing a very steep mountain and that, like those people in mountain climbing documentaries, we eat and sleep on the side of the mountain; we can never get off or take a break. This part of the journey feels totally overwhelming: so much to learn and so much to do. You may think you have to do it all right now and support your child in every area right this minute.

In the past, when you've had a long list of urgent tasks, what happened? Did you efficiently work through them one by one?

More likely, this list paralysed you and made it impossible for you to move forward. If you crossed even one thing off the list, that would have been quite an accomplishment.

This is precisely how it is with everything you feel you need to do for your child. When you realize your child is autistic, you become acutely aware of the many ways they are different to or behind their same-age peers. It's normal to feel an urgent need to help your child in all of the areas where they are lagging. You might create a plan that involves doing several things every day to help your child with every aspect of life. I must admit that I did this, too, having a daily list that included sensory activities, speech therapy, deep pressure and even Chinese massage. I didn't do any of it!

I'm sorry to tell you that trying to tackle everything at once is a recipe for failure. First, autism doesn't often play nicely with our plans, timekeeping or moving forward in a linear fashion. Autism does what it likes. It's vital to your child's wellbeing and happiness (and yours, too) that you focus on one thing at a time. Just toileting. Just getting dressed. Just sorting out school issues.

When you just focus on just one thing, you give yourself the freedom to explore that matter in depth. What do you need to know about toilet training an autistic child? Why is your child struggling with this issue? How can you help them? Is now the right time to pursue this, or should you leave it?

More importantly, you give your child time to learn something new without pressure. Our children learn differently to non-autistic children and differently to each other. Take time to find your child's learning style and what works for them. Are they a visual learner? Do they like watching videos of how to do things or having a visual guide? Do they prefer simply being told what to do? Would they rather read about how to do something? These are all questions to explore with your child.

The fear of getting it wrong may also paralyse you into inaction. You may have times when you feel like you don't know what you are doing. This may even be several times a day. That's OK! It's during these times that the greatest innovation occurs. The key is to try something anyway, and if that doesn't work, try something else. Be extremely patient; just keep trying and you will get there. It may feel like nothing you try works, which can be a knock to your confidence. However, this is how you learn. It's crucial to go with your gut instinct here because it is always right. If your gut instinct says to try something, try it! You will find your way with your child. When you get something right, it will be a huge win and you'll feel like a genius.

Be sure to celebrate small wins as well. Since the beginning of the Covid pandemic (March 2020), I have been working with my daughter to help her dress herself. As I type, it is December 2022 and we are still working on this. I have celebrated along the way when she hit wondrous milestones like putting on her shoes and beginning to do and undo her own buttons. We've got a way to go but great progress has been made.

Worry and fear take up a lot of brain space and time. It's easy to waste time worrying instead of taking action. I drive my daughter to school, it's a long drive, and one day I happened to notice that there were planned roadworks on the route we take to school for the next ten days. Stopping in traffic for any reason upsets my daughter in a big way. I let myself get super stressed about these roadworks and spent over an hour trying to plan a different route to school. However, I realized that this was doing neither of us any favours. Instead of going a different route to avoid the roadworks, I created a visual for my daughter to explain that sometimes we get stuck in traffic jams or have to stop at traffic lights, and this is OK. This morning I gave her the visual and talked her through it when we got in the car. I drove my normal route, got stuck at the temporary traffic light for the roadworks and guess what? She was fine. Sometimes we have to get out of the fear and just get on with it.

The spiky profile

Autistic individuals have what is called a spiky profile. This means that they will excel in some areas, like playing the piano or reading, but struggle in others, like dressing themselves or using the toilet independently. This can be very confusing for a parent as it is difficult to understand why something that *for you* is complicated (like playing the piano) is easier for your child than something that *for you* is very simple (like using the toilet). Again, this is why it is important to just work on one area at a time and see how it goes. If it's not possible for your child to address that issue at that time, just move on.

Now that I've shared that important preamble, let's get stuck in to the Big Five.

CHAPTER 12

Executive Functioning

Almost all neurodivergent individuals struggle with something called executive functioning. Executive functioning is our ability to plan, organize ourselves for and carry out tasks. It involves making decisions about what is needed, what order to do things in and what to do if things go wrong.

What may seem like a simple task like getting dressed for school may feel to an autistic child like an insurmountable set of decisions and actions. If you think of all that's involved in just getting dressed, you'll see what I mean:

1. Choose what to wear.

2. Is it cold/rainy/hot outside?

3. What shirt should I wear?

4. What trousers should I wear?

5. What underwear should I wear?

6. What shoes should I wear?

7. If I need a jumper, what jumper should I wear?

8. Remember to take current clothes off.

9. Remember to put current clothes in the washing basket.

10. Find the chosen clothes for the day.

11. Put on the chosen clothes for the day.

12. What order do these things go in?

13. Do these things go together?

14. Does this shirt/jumper/pair of trousers still fit me?

That's a lot of thought that must go into this task. This level of decision making in a short period of time may feel overwhelming to your child.

Here is another dressing-related example. A friend of mine has a daughter who is about 11 years old. My friend puts her daughter's school clothes out in the order that they need to be put on. One day, her daughter decided to get dressed in the bathroom instead of her bedroom. She picked up the stack of clothes to take into the bathroom, but in doing so, she jumbled them out of order. When she came down for breakfast, she was wearing her bra top over her school shirt, and she didn't know this wasn't right because that was the order things had been in when she got dressed.

For further explanation, I'll also share my adult executive functioning conundrum: posting greeting cards. In order to do this successfully, I have to:

- remember the birthday

- buy the card

- write in the card

- find the person's address

- find a stamp or, more likely, buy stamps

- find a postbox that collects before the end of the day because I'll have left posting the card until the last minute.

It's not just doing all of these seemingly small and easy things. Putting these steps together is actually hard for me. What has helped me with this is creating a card box where I keep spare greeting cards, stamps and a pen. I put everyone's birthday on the calendar in my phone and also make sure I have people's addresses on my phone as well. You can do this kind of thing for your child too, putting things together that they will need for certain tasks to help them stay organized.

I'm telling you all of this because if you don't understand that your child has issues with executive functioning, you may get extremely frustrated with what appears to be your child's wilful lack of interest in getting dressed for school and thus, you may go through some truly stressful times together. Children always want to do well and they will succeed with the right tools for the job.

Non-autistic children learn by watching and copying those around them – their parents, siblings and peers. Autistic children do some of this, but generally have to be taught *everything*. This can be a long, slow process and requires enormous patience. Life is generally more challenging for your autistic child than for a non-autistic child. Sensory issues, cognitive and communication delays can seriously impact on a child's ability to master what might otherwise be thought of as a simple task. Please don't get caught up in feeling like your child isn't trying hard enough or that you aren't doing enough. The mindset with our children isn't 'how do I *get* my child to...' but 'how can I *help* my child to...' How can you make tasks simpler for your child? How can you support your child?

The way to support your child with executive functioning issues is to teach them the steps for everything. That sounds daunting, doesn't it? I'm sorry to say this really is the way forward. Use visual schedules to help them get ready for school or ready for bed. Provide lists of the steps needed. Use something called 'chaining' to help them gain independence.

How to use chaining

Chaining is a technique that can help children (of all ages) learn new skills and routines. With chaining, you are talking the child through how to execute a certain task, prompting them with words and/or visuals about what the next step is.

For example, using chaining to teach a child how to dress for school could involve:

1. Take off pyjamas and pants.

2. Put on clean pants.

3. Put on trousers.

4. Put on school shirt.

5. Put on jumper/tie/blazer.

6. Put on socks.

7. Put on shoes.

With a list or visual representation of the above, you can prompt the child to complete the 'chain' of activity. Ask, 'what do we do first?' then, 'what do we do next?' and repeat until finished. Completing this exercise daily will enable the child to learn the steps needed to do this task independently.

Depending on the cognitive ability of your child, you may need to break each step down further for understanding. For example, putting on a shirt has several steps:

1. Put shirt over head.

2. Make sure it's the right way round.

3. Put right arm through right shirt sleeve.

4. Put left arm through left shirt sleeve.

5. Pull shirt down.

6. Button shirt buttons.

Focus on one step at a time until the child can do the task independently.

I use this with my daughter in a lot of different situations. When getting dressed for school, I have all of her clothes ready and will prompt her every step of the way. 'What do you need to do first?' 'Can you find your shirt?' 'Where is your jacket? Please put on your jacket,' and so on. My friend Bea first used chaining to teach her son how to put on his socks, shoes and jacket, as these were things he would need to be able to do at school.

I also put my daughter's clothes in one of those hanging clothing storage systems that has seven large compartments. I've used double-sided tape to stick laminated day labels on each section. This helps develop one more step of independence as she can get all of the clothing for any given day herself. (You can buy ready-made day-labelled storage systems, too.)

How to use visuals to support your child

Many autistic individuals are visual learners. Using visuals can help to:

- lead them through a particular task

- understand what to expect

- understand what is expected of them

- reduce anxiety

- understand what is happening now, next and later

- take the onus off you to nag them to do things.

Visual tools are helpful no matter what age your child is. Even if you have a teenager, visuals can help them stay organized and gain independence.

You can use visuals in all sorts of ways. You can make them yourself, or buy them ready-made. It's important not to get hung up on the pictures being perfect, or an exact image of what you are hoping to communicate. Children respond well to simple symbols and even hand-drawn images. Even a basic stick man figure holding a cup to indicate 'drink' will work for most children.

When my daughter was nonspeaking, I went way over the top with creating visuals. I took pictures of every toy, every article of clothing, every game on the iPad, every television show, and so on. (This was autistic rigid thinking in action!) You don't need to do this. Just basic images that are symbolic will do. For example, one image that represents 'toys' and one image that represents 'eating' will work for starters.

A *visual routine* helps a child work out what to do and in what order. Again, you can buy these ready-made or make them yourself. A visual routine for something like getting ready for bed would include, in order of how they are meant to be done, things like brushing teeth, taking a bath, putting on pyjamas, getting into bed, reading a story and lights out. You can use visual routines for anything that has steps to follow.

A *'now and next' board* helps a child understand what is happening. It is simpler than a full visual routine and just focuses on what is happening now and next. For example, now we are washing our hands, then we are eating lunch and after that we are going to the playground.

You can use images you take yourself to create a *visual sequence*. I find this helps my daughter make sense of what's needed. I took pictures of her washing her hands and created a visual sequence that I've stuck on the bathroom wall above the sink to remind her of what to do and in what order.

Social stories can be very helpful for curbing negative behaviours. If you have a child who screams when they are upset, you can create a social story that gives other options for how they can manage their upset besides screaming. For example, the visual might say, 'when I get angry, I scream! Instead of screaming, I could: play the piano, draw a picture, play with the dog, blow some bubbles, listen to music, take some deep breaths or ask for a hug'.

Another great tool for creating visuals is something called *The Incredible Five Point Scale*. This is a scale you can use for many different situations. For example, if you have an anxious child, 'one' on the scale could be calm and happy and 'five' could be extremely anxious. You may choose to use colours instead, so that blue is calm and happy and red is extremely anxious and the colours in between show an increase in anxiety. You can use the scale in many ways. I use it to help my daughter understand that she does not need to play the piano at full volume ('five' on the scale) but it would be much better to stay nearer to 'one' or 'two'.

Depending on your child, you may not need visuals at all. In some situations, my daughter is very happy to have a written list of what is happening and what to expect. We read the list together and tick things off as we go along.

You'll find examples of the above ideas and lots of links for free and paid-for visual resources at wdisbook.com/resources.

It's important to understand that when you first hand your child a visual schedule or timetable, they may react badly. Even though a visual device will help them, it's still a change that must be assimilated into their life. They may tear it up, throw it on the floor, or hide it in a drawer. Don't despair. Just print out another one for them. They will very likely come to accept and even appreciate it in time.

If/then

Executive functioning also involves knowing what to do if things don't go to plan. This can be very difficult for our children as it involves a change of plans or routine. As we know, life is full of unexpected things, swimming pool closures, roadworks, not having all of the ingredients for the cake, and so on. Helping our children find workarounds for life's unforeseen obstacles is hugely important. Help your child understand 'if *this* happens, then we will do *that* instead' so that they understand that all is not lost if things don't go to plan. It's generally worth having a plan B, C and D.

Help your child develop independence

If you have a child who struggles with self-care such as getting dressed or personal hygiene tasks, you need to do everything you can to help them to do these things themselves. I know very well how hard it is to be patient when you are in a rush to get out the door to school or somewhere else. When it takes your child 20 minutes to dress themselves when you could dress them in five, it's tempting to just do it yourself. However, remember this chilling fact: your child will outlive you. You may not be around to dress them when they are 30 or 40 so you'll want to be getting on with supporting them in doing this for themselves now.

Getting your head round executive functioning and all the ways you need to support your child with it takes time. At first it will feel like a lot of work. However, once your child begins to make strides and things start to get easier, you will both start feeling a lot more confident. As with many things I cover in this book, with executive functioning, you just need to pick a starting place and go for it.

CHAPTER 13

Anxiety

Autistic people are anxious people. Statistics about the number of anxious autistic people vary widely, from around 20 per cent to 84 per cent. In my experience, just about all autistic people experience anxiety on a regular basis.

What is causing the anxiety?

A few years ago, I was driving my daughter home from school and I said that we had to go to the post office on the way home. She became very upset by this. I quickly realized that I had not taken her to a post office for many years, and she did not understand what the words 'post office' meant. I stopped the car, got a piece of paper and wrote out for her what was going to happen at the post office. She then had a short checklist of what to expect and how she would know when we were finished and she was happy to carry on.

Remember that our children don't know what they don't know. We must explain to them what to expect and what is expected of them. Here are just a few things that may cause anxiety, especially when your child is away from home: at school, going on holiday, visiting a new shop, at Scout camp and so on:

- What am I supposed to do in this situation? What is expected of me? What am I supposed to wear or take with me? Do I have to do anything, or can I just be there? What do I need to do before I go there?

- What if I look stupid because I don't know what to do?

- What if there is a sensory issue (bright light, bad smell, messy play, and so on) that will upset me?

- What if I throw up in front of everyone? (A surprisingly common worry amongst autistic children.)

- What if I need the toilet and I can't find one or there isn't one or I can't get to the toilet on time?

- What happens first, second, last at this place?

- Who will be there? Will I know anyone? Will there be someone I don't like there?

All these points are to do with unclear expectations: what will happen, what am I meant to do, what do I wear, what if so and so is there, and so on. This also ties in with rumination – which means thinking about something obsessively over a period of time, generally in a negative way. If your child knows there is an event or activity coming up and they don't know what is expected of them or what to expect, they may be thinking quite a lot about this. Be sure to tell your child that they will come home from the event or activity, as otherwise they may not understand this is the case and they may think they are going away but not coming back. This worry may result in distress behaviours that at first glance may not appear to be related to the event or activity.

These worries are also about being out of control, which is a huge cause of anxiety for autistic individuals. It can lead to demand avoidance and/or generally finding unhealthy ways to be in control such as avoiding washing, restrictive eating, refusing school or requiring rigid routines that other family members also must take part in.

The behaviour iceberg

As a parent of an autistic child, you will often see a visual representation of behaviour in the form of an iceberg. The point of the visual, no pun intended, is that what you can see in your child's behaviour is just the tip of the iceberg, and underneath the water are the causes of the behaviour (hunger, shame, confusion, disappointment, boredom, unexpected transition, sensory overload, and so on), and anxiety is at the centre. Anxiety is the number one cause of distress for autistic people. Autistic people are anxious by nature. An autistic person's anxiety is on a different level than the average person and autistic people are anxious more of the time than a typical person.

Shame causes anxiety. Boredom causes anxiety. If your child has more than one thing going on, for example, hunger, confusion, and an inability to communicate their distress, their anxiety will be high.

Signs that your child may be anxious

- Controlling behaviour, lack of compromise, inflexibility
- problems with leaving the house or getting to school
- ruminating and catastrophizing
- tummy aches and headaches
- obsessive behaviours or rituals
- an intense need to stick to routines
- aggression and physical behaviours
- running away
- sleep issues
- self-harm
- repetitive behaviours.

It's important that you see that anxiety is often at the core of these behaviours so that you don't punish your child but instead seek to soothe their anxiety. Anxiety may lead to difficult behaviour, but it's crucial to remember this point: your child is not giving you a hard time; they are having a hard time. Your support of your anxious child begins with compassion about their behaviour and understanding that they truly don't want to behave 'badly' but their anxiety leads them to act out in a variety of challenging ways.

RUMINATION

Rumination is the act of thinking about something negative over and over. Autistic people are especially prone to rumination. When we have an unpleasant experience, see something upsetting, or someone has made a comment that makes us anxious, we often think about this for a very long time afterwards.

I have learned how to manage rumination in my life. For example, if a colleague says something that upsets me, or I've watched a distressing scene on television, thoughts about these situations will spin round and round in my head for a long time. I have developed the emotional regulation skills to switch off these thoughts after a short period of time. Autistic children often lack this ability and will ruminate about something for an excessively long time, even years.

Rumination is very difficult for the people around the ruminator to understand. It can also be confusing for parents as it may not be apparent that your child is doing it. They may seem unsettled but are unable to communicate what has happened. It may take some time before your child talks about what they are ruminating about. I know of children who began talking about a traumatic event weeks or even years after the fact but made no mention of it at the time it happened.

The benefit of rumination is that it enables the person doing it to look at a situation from every angle, inside and out. By doing this, we can potentially work out why it happened and possibly how to prevent such a thing from happening in the future. Again, children may lack the skills to dissect a situation to glean this kind of knowledge.

It's important to understand that rumination is likely part of your child's life. If your child seems upset but can't express what is happening to them, some leading questions might help unpick the issue. Try asking them specifically about things that you know have happened, for example, a medical appointment, school field trip or a visit to a relative's house. Asking your child directly what is upsetting them may help them to open up as well. It may be easier for them to write out what is troubling them instead of having to talk about it.

A trick that works for me when I find myself ruminating is to do what I call 'switching the visual'. This involves replacing an unpleasant thought or scene with a pleasant one. If I have seen something disturbing, I push the image away by imagining a pleasant scene, like a beach or flower garden. If my rumination involves another person, I replace the negative thoughts with positive ones, such as having fun with my daughter. It has taken practice to remember to do this, but it is an effective way to move on from rumination. Another trick for getting out of rumination is to imagine the unpleasant scene on a giant screen, and to visualize taking a squeegee to wipe it away or throwing a giant stone at the screen to smash it into pieces.

Social anxiety

Most autistic people suffer from social anxiety in some way. I've made a point to dive a bit deeper into this type of anxiety as it affects our children so pervasively.

What is social anxiety?

Every person is different but many with social anxiety experience a fear of being around people they don't know well and going to new places. Perfectionism can be an issue, with the person putting huge pressure on themselves to be flawless. Social anxiety sufferers worry excessively about what other people, strangers especially, think of them. Some people with this type of anxiety have selective mutism, which prevents them from speaking in public (at school, for example).

What does it look like?

Social anxiety can cause the sufferer to fear leaving the house. This may be a gradual reduction in outings or a sudden stop. They may worry excessively that other people are looking at them, talking about them or thinking about them in a negative way. Social anxiety causes extreme self-consciousness. A person with it will worry constantly that other people are focused on them when they are not.

Social anxiety can have a major impact on a child at school. They may avoid answering questions or speaking at all in class because they are so afraid of saying the wrong thing or getting an answer wrong (even if they know it's right). Similarly, a child with social anxiety may not join a sports team for fear of not doing well. They may resist trying new activities, for example, a club at school based on a favourite topic. Kids with social anxiety struggle to engage with other children, even when the other children want to engage with them. Additionally, a child with social anxiety may not eat or drink in public, as these activities are fraught with potential disasters of spilling something on themselves or getting food on their face. An individual with social anxiety may choose to avoid doing this as the worry about the potential of these things happening is too great.

The social anxiety sufferer may be unable to leave the house unless their appearance, hair, makeup and clothing are exactly as they require it to be. This issue seems to afflict girls more than boys, possibly because there is more pressure on girls to 'fit in' with clothing and other fashion trends. It can lead to enormous stress in trying to get ready for school because if one detail of her appearance isn't just right, she may be paralysed by anxiety and unable to leave the house.

Social anxiety is totally illogical, irrational and confusing. I know this because I suffered with social anxiety for most of my life. It is nearly impossible for the people around the sufferer of it to understand. The person struggling with it will do all kinds of things that may look very strange and even bizarre to the people around them. For example:

- the child who won't leave the house for school because their shoes are not exactly perfect or they cannot find their lip gloss

- the child who hides in the footwell of the passenger seat when you are going somewhere because they are extremely worried that people are looking at them

- the teenager who hides under a hooded top or coat year round so as not to be seen by anyone (sometimes this is a sensory need but sometimes it is also anxiety).

What's at the heart of social anxiety?

Social anxiety is driven by the individual's intense belief that they are not good enough. There is also often an extreme level of perfectionism that rides alongside this belief. This is why it feels like the end of the world for the girl who can't find her lip gloss before school.

Autism can make social anxiety even more deeply embedded because of struggles with social understanding. Autistic people have social deficits. These will lessen over time, but autistic children are often keenly aware of their differences and know they don't always or often get things right socially. Black and white/all or nothing thinking such as, 'I had a bad experience once, therefore all similar experiences will be bad' can make anxiety worse. Children also have immature logic which can further entrench this kind of thinking because they simply lack the life experience to know better.

Emotional dysregulation causes our kids to feel things far more intensely than typical children do. Something that might be a bit embarrassing for a typical child might be crushing for an autistic one. Additionally, rumination is a factor here as well. An autistic child may have a bad experience or make a social faux pas and then ruminate about this for months or even years after the fact. The situation may grow in negativity and intensity in their mind far beyond what actually took place.

What causes social anxiety?

The transition out of childhood can be a factor in social anxiety. Up until the age of seven or eight, children play with toys. As typical children get older, they become more interested in socializing. While your child may have fit in with their peers in Reception, Year One and Year Two (around age four to age seven), after that their interests may not be the same. This can cause social isolation and anxiety.

People with social anxiety worry about letting people down. If your child is worried about letting an important adult in their life down, they may choose to avoid taking part in any activity where this might happen. For example, if a family holiday has been planned, a child with social anxiety may do just about anything to get out of this for fear of disappointing the family.

There is also some evidence that anxiety disorders may be inherited from parents or grandparents. If you suffer from anxiety, it will be especially important for you to watch out for this in your child.

Masking and anxiety

Masking is a survival strategy for autistic people. It is a way for an individual to become someone entirely different to their true self. In essence, they are hiding their true self because they believe there is something wrong with the way they are naturally. Autistic people mask as a way to reduce the anxiety they feel when they are out in the world and around other people.

Everyone, autistic or not, engages in masking of some sort. For example, a non-autistic person who is anxious about a meeting at work may put on a brave face to get through it. For autistic people, masking is far more intense and it's nearly constant. An autistic person may mask every time they are in a social situation or at school, while a non-autistic person only does it some of the time.

The first rule about masking is that we have to talk about masking. Autistic children who mask do it unconsciously – they don't realize they are doing it. Even if they are spending all their free time studying popular music, games, clothes, and so on, they won't know that this is masking. They will think that everyone is doing this and that this is what is required to get through life.

Some people use the term 'camouflaging' instead of 'masking'. However, I feel that 'camouflaging' is a passive state, where the person is trying to be invisible in order to go unnoticed, but 'masking' is an active state, where the person is purposefully trying to fit in.

Only girls mask, right?

Wrong. It is fair to say that a higher percentage of autistic girls mask than autistic boys. Some girls may be more aware of and care more about being accepted by other girls. Society also puts huge pressure on girls to conform, be nice, be good, be quiet, and so on. Boys definitely mask. This stereotype causes problems because some parents and professionals may not believe a boy is masking. Similarly, not every girl masks.

What's wrong with masking?

Your child is making friends, doing well at school and enjoying a lot of different activities. What's wrong with that? This is a delicate topic, especially if you are fairly new to autism. Used in the right context, masking can be very helpful. As I mentioned above, it is a self-preservation method and it can help an autistic person get through situations that make them anxious. The trouble is that masking does what it says on the tin. It hides the person's real self from the world and presents a false version instead.

Of course, it is possible for an autistic child to make friends, do well at school and enjoy a lot of different activities. However, masking is such an intrinsic part of autism that it will always be important to keep it in mind. Look at how your child is behaving in different scenarios outside of the house as opposed to how they are at home. If there is a big disconnect between the two, you have a problem. So, for example, if your child seems happy when he is spending time with friends but very unhappy at home. Or, if when they get home from school, they either blow up or shut down, they are likely to be masking at school.

Another issue with masking is that it's hard to maintain. Your child may have just enough social skill to make a good first impression but nothing further. They may understand that they need to say, 'hello, how are you?' but they don't know that they need to wait for the person they've asked to answer. Or they may chameleon their way into a friendship or social group, believing that they can lose the fake persona after a while and the friend or group will still like them, but this may not be what actually happens.

Why do children mask?

A child will start masking if they realize that if they act differently to their natural self:

- they seem to fit in better with other children

- their family members are happier

- their teachers are not annoyed with them

- life is generally easier.

Even a very young child understands cause and effect: if I do this, this happens and if I do that, that happens. If you have a young child who realizes that if they flap and hum other children ignore them, but when they keep still and quiet they are included in games, it's easy to see how the seed of masking is planted. Similarly, if they flap and hum and Grandad angrily tells them to stop, they will.

There are many reasons an autistic person masks, but anxiety is always at the core of masking. Sometimes the reasons are place- or person-specific, for example at school or when they are with a certain friend or relative.

Autistic people, children especially, mask to fly under the radar of the people around them. If the child lives in a volatile household or has a volatile teacher, they may mask to make themselves invisible and to keep the peace. Masking helps children please the people in their lives, for example, 'Grandad shouts at me when I hum and flap so I won't do that around Grandad and then Grandad will like me'.

Masking can help a child to make friends. The masker is the best friend ever! They will do whatever the other child wants, take up their interests, go where they want to go. This is exhausting and impossible to keep up for very long.

A tricky thing about masking is that it can act like useful false courage, or a sort of fake-it-till-you-make it tool. If a person needs to be a certain way to get a job, get the part in the school play or win a competition, then masking can be helpful. With something like getting a job, masking may not be great as the person will need to keep up the act and actually do what they have claimed they can in order to be successful (this I know from painful life experience).

Another important aspect of masking is that autistic people mask because society tells them that being autistic is a bad thing. This is a sad fact but very true. The media tells us to embrace our true selves but society doesn't really want that. Society loves conformity. Autism and conformity are chalk and cheese.

Examples of masking

Scripting and rehearsing conversations and jokes
Sometimes the material for this kind of thing comes from television or films, so the potential for getting it wrong is high as the person may not understand the context of the conversation and try to apply one conversation to a wide range of situations.

Playing past conversations over and over in their head to find ways to improve in the future
This is very stressful as they may beat themselves up for getting a minor detail wrong, like tone of voice or using the wrong word for something.

Memorizing social scripts to engage appropriately in 'small talk'
Autistic people are very efficient. Small talk to an autistic person is like wasted air. However, it is part of society and unless a person can take part, they may look odd or rude, so an autistic person will memorize standard small talk fare. For example, 'what did you do at the weekend?' 'the weather is terrible (or lovely) isn't it?' and so on, and also memorize reasonable answers in case someone asks them questions like this.

Researching topics they think might appeal to the people they are mimicking
For example, popular video games, television shows, bands, and so on.

Studying others around them to copy every detail of clothing style, ways of speaking and laughing, body language, facial expressions, etc.
The trouble with this is that these are nuanced things with unspoken reasons and meanings. It takes relentless studying and practice to get these kinds of things right, especially for children. An added

difficulty is that sometimes popular fashion is out of the price range of the child's family but instead of just leaving it they may try to cobble a look together that really doesn't work.

Forcing themselves to make eye contact

Eye contact is a hot topic in the autistic world. Many autistic people find eye contact extremely uncomfortable and prefer instead to look at someone's forehead or mouth. Some non-autistic people make a big fuss about eye contact and believe that if a person is not making eye contact with them that they are not listening or are being rude. They may even say things like, 'look at me when I am speaking to you'. The message that not making eye contact is a bad thing is prevalent in schools and sometimes at home as well. It's no wonder that children will force themselves to make eye contact in order to fit in and/or keep the peace.

Suppressing 'autisticness'

For example, not:

- letting on when they have sensory difficulties, for example when a room is too bright or too loud

- using sensory supports like ear defenders

- wearing adapted school uniform in order to be more comfortable

- engaging in or talking about favourite activities

    They may be aware that other children are not interested in their specialist topic or that their favourite toys are considered 'babyish' by their peers, so they'll keep those things well hidden.

- stimming

    Stimming is short for 'self-stimulatory behaviours' and includes things like flapping, humming, spinning, playing with a piece of string, chewing the collar of their shirt. These are calming activities that an individual engages in to self soothe, and I would never advise that they be stopped from doing so unless the activity was harmful (more on this in Chapter 15). The child may stop stimming altogether or they may do something more subtle but far less satisfying and effective, such as playing with their hair or simply fidgeting.

- engaging in echolalia.

  Echolalia is where the person repeats a word or phrase over and over. Sometimes this is a soothing thing and sometimes it is just how the person communicates. If an individual is aware that this behaviour isn't approved of by others they may stop, but this could cut them off from something calming or a method of self-expression (more on this in Chapter 16).

Really working at fitting in
For example, by:

- taking on hobbies or sports they have no interest in

- listening to music they don't enjoy

- watching television shows they don't like watching

- going to places they don't want to go

- wearing things (popular clothing, shoes and/or makeup) that make them uncomfortable

- spending time with people they don't like or who make them uncomfortable

- saying 'yes' to things that don't feel right for them

- hugging people when touch is uncomfortable for them

just so that they can 'look the part' and speak fluently about these things with their peers. Reading through this list, you can see why helping your child to stop or reduce masking is essential as they get older.

How do you know if your child is masking?

The older a person is, the harder it will be to tell if they are masking or not, as masking is a skill that, like any, improves over time. Girls appear to be exceptionally good at masking. Again, this may be because society puts pressure on girls to be 'nice' and 'good' (even if parents do not do this at home), and so they are actively striving to fit in and hide their true selves and feelings.

If your child is engaging in things you know they don't enjoy, and/or you know they struggle with social situations but they are still taking part in activities, they are likely masking in order to do this. If your child says things like, 'I want to fit in but don't know how', or 'I don't want anyone to think I'm weird', they may mask to fit in with their peers. A child whose interaction with others appears wooden, unnatural or over the top, especially in unfamiliar environments is likely masking.

If you don't know whether or not your child is masking, they probably are. Listen to your parental gut.

The negative impact of masking

Masking causes overload. Imagine a child at school, pretending to be OK with the noise, hustle and bustle, chairs scraping against the floor, and so on. They may have also been holding themselves together through confusion and feeling different to the other children. By the end of the day, they are totally overloaded. They leave school and either meltdown or shutdown. Over time, masking can completely deplete a person's mental reserves. They may go from needing a bit of time to themselves after school to extreme burnout.

As I've mentioned, it takes autistic children much longer to learn emotional and sensory regulation skills than it does their non-autistic peers. If a child is masking by pretending that lights, sounds and smells aren't bothering them, they will most certainly become overloaded and meltdowns or shutdowns will be more common.

Masking can result in isolation, low confidence and self-esteem, anxiety and depression. If a child has been masking to fit in with a social group or another child, but they can't keep it up, that group or child will understandably think the child is a bit strange and may move away from them. They may even make fun of or bully the child. Also, if a child has been working desperately hard to fit in but still hasn't, this can be very upsetting. They may feel like, 'I've worked so hard; why don't I have any friends?'

Masking can lead to poor self-awareness. If a person is masking all the time they will have a difficult time working out what they actually do like. If they are pretending to like Minecraft, Harry Styles, and whatever else, they may not realize they actually like archaeology and Mozart.

How can you help your child to stop masking?

First and foremost, you need to be absolutely, 100 per cent sure that you are in no way the cause of your child masking. This is so important! This is not meant to make you feel uncomfortable but if it does, then it's likely something you need to look at and adjust in yourself.

I've said this elsewhere, but it bears repeating: when your child hears you speak negatively about getting support for them at school, the long wait for assessment, and/or people who look or act differently to society's 'normal', it's possible and indeed likely that they will feel that they have somehow caused your irritation. If they weren't different, you wouldn't have to go through any of these things and you wouldn't be stressed or upset about them. Children internalize the messages that they hear from us. Even when we think they are not listening, they definitely are, so it's vital to be very mindful of when and where you vent your feelings about negative things that are happening. Also, be mindful of who you talk to as you don't want your vented thoughts or worries to get back to your child via another source.

What can you do to help your child with anxiety?

If your child is suffering from anxiety, helping them will require you to be patient. This is an understatement. What I want you to do is develop a deep level of patience beyond what you have ever had before. You must find a way to be patient about the lip gloss or the shoes or inability to get in the car or out of the car or however anxiety manifests for your son or daughter. You need to be compassionate and understand that your child doesn't want to be this way. The anxiety they are feeling is real and causing them huge distress. The things they are anxious about may seem silly to you but they aren't to them. Empathy and sensitivity are required here.

Anxiety is very difficult to cope with as a parent but remember it is far more difficult and painful for the child. If a parent reacts angrily to a child who is struggling in this way, it will make things worse. Children must know they can depend on the adults around them to love them unconditionally even when their behaviour is very challenging.

If you are a parent who has shouted at your child when they are struggling with anxiety, please understand that I have not given you this information so that you have a new stick to beat yourself with. You didn't know then what you know now. Now you can get on with doing things in a new way and make up for the past.

What specific strategies can you use with anxiety?

What you choose to do is very personal and will depend on your resources and current family situation. There is no one right way to help your child. Below are some ideas to think about.

Visual schedules and coaching

As much as possible, explain clearly what is happening and what is expected of your child. Use visual guides, visual schedules, lists or anything else you feel will work for them. I create a fortnightly visual schedule for my daughter that gets updated weekly. It is posted on the door to our living room so that it is always available for her to look at. It's not fancy, just a Word document that explains where she is throughout each week (at school, at her dad's, and so on).

When something out of the ordinary happens, for example, a medical appointment or a big change at school, I create visual guides that explain exactly what will happen. We recently had separate visits for an X-ray and a blood draw at our local hospital. For each of these, I created very clear visual guides that I gave to her a week in advance. The appointments were also on her schedule. I sat down with her and talked her through each procedure. I printed a copy for her to have at home and one for the car so that she could review them whenever she wanted to.

Using guides like this is a way of coaching a child through what might be a stressful experience. By providing clear information well in advance you can reduce your child's anxiety dramatically.

Take a break

If your child is seriously struggling with a particular activity, let them take a break from it. This is very subjective. Some parents will feel that a child must persevere to gain new life and social skills and they must learn to work through things. Others will feel it's cruel to force a child to do something they simply cannot cope with. There's no right answer here, but my suggestion would be to err on the side of mental health. You won't be stopping something forever, just until your child feels more able to cope. This could be on a smaller scale, for example not making them go to family activities or birthday parties, or on a bigger scale, such as having your GP sign your child off school because of anxiety. These are not easy decisions so it's down to what your parental gut tells you is right.

Forward plan

What will your child need in order to cope with a particular activity? What are they going to need to get ready for school tomorrow? By planning and thinking things through, you can save a lot of drama. If you can ensure the lip gloss is where it's meant to be the night before, you are more likely to have a smoother journey from home to school.

Pre-catastrophize with them

This may sound counterintuitive but if you help your child to see the difference between what they are afraid of and what is actually probable this can help to shift their perspective. In a gently compassionate (and never condescending!) way, ask, 'what's the worst thing that can happen?' and talk through the answers. If for example, they feel the worst thing that can happen is that all of their clothes will fall off, they will be sick and break wind all at the same time, you can help them see that, although some of these things are possible they are not likely and certainly not all at the same time. Once you've got to a potentially possible vision of the 'worst thing that can happen' with your child, then the question is 'so what?' for example if your child is fixated on being sick in public, talk about what would happen if this did occur. In this scenario, it's likely that all the children would immediately be taken out of the room and the sick would be cleaned up and life would go on. By talking things through in advance we can gently help our kids see the loopholes in their anxiety-fuelling fears. It also helps build trust by talking things through as it will show you are taking their worries seriously enough to want to help.

Give more time
Factor into the schedule time for upset and time to calm down. Autism and social anxiety are enemies of time management. You need to allow time for your child to work through whatever they are dealing with. I factor in an extra hour before school to allow for upset and recovery time.

Be realistic
This works with giving more time. For example, don't assume you are going to run a bunch of crucial errands while out with your socially anxious son or daughter and then still get to where you are going on time. Another example is to not leave something you need to do until the last minute as your child's need for your time and comfort may well get in the way of this. Plan in advance what needs doing and be realistic about what your child can cope with and what time you'll need to give them.

Get help
If your child is experiencing anxiety in any form for more than a few months, you should seek help. The waiting lists for CAMHS are

very long, and it's possible that the help provided will not be of use. However, there are mental health charities you may be able to get affordable help from. You may need to pay privately for therapy for your child. Many therapists offer sliding fee scales if cost is an issue.

Improve your child's self-esteem

Low confidence and poor self-esteem will have a huge impact on your child's mental health and can lead to behaviours you may find challenging. Our children are dealing with all sorts of difficult things such as shame and knowing that they don't fit in. Again, rumination is an issue as a child may go over social mishaps again and again, which also impacts on self-esteem and confidence.

Self-esteem is made up of a person's view of their own self-worth, value and their place in the world. It also encompasses an individual's assessment and valuation of their own appearance, world view, personality, behaviour, and so on, as well as beliefs and perceptions about how others see them.

What causes low self-esteem?

Autistic children have a lot going on that may have a negative impact on self-esteem. They may see themselves as different to or 'less than' their peers, and may believe they are not as good, clever, strong, and so on as other children. The fact that autistic children may be excluded from social events and parties will exacerbate these beliefs. Frustration and/or embarrassment about social difficulties will create problems, and a child may see their differences as deficits.

They may think that they are 'weird' and that no one else has the same worries as they do. For a child with poor self-esteem, the glass is always half empty as they focus on their personal challenges instead of strengths. As I've mentioned before, perfectionism can be an issue for our children, and a child may believe that if they can't do something perfectly, there's no point doing it at all. Unrealistic expectations of themselves and others may be an issue. Adding a further layer of difficulty, they may take suggestions as criticism and criticism as a personal attack.

It's important to note that if your child is seeing a lot of different professionals (assessment team, speech and language therapist, occupational therapist, etc.), as can sometimes be the case, they may think this means they are broken and need fixing. If it's possible with your child, ensure that you explain appointments and the role of professionals clearly to avoid misunderstandings.

How can you help your child improve their self-esteem?

First and foremost: be a good role model. If your own self-esteem is poor, you will struggle to help your child improve theirs. You may need to do some work in this area for your efforts to be effective.

Focus on the positive aspects of autism and not just the challenges. Talk about famous autistic people; there seem to be more celebrities 'coming out' as autistic now than ever before. It's important for your child to see that autism isn't a 'life sentence' but just a different way of being in the world, and that success and happiness is possible. Normalize autism and neurodiversity. Talk about it openly with your child. Welcome differences and uniqueness. Disability of all kinds is no longer hidden away as it was 40 or 50 years ago. We now see disabled people on television, in sports, films and most importantly, out and about in the world.

Help your child to be realistic about what they and others can achieve. Expecting themselves or you to be able to draw Marvel comic characters like a professional illustrator is not realistic, but you may have fun drawing a lot of other things together. Teach your child that mistakes are OK and this is how everyone learns new skills. Celebrate attempts and not just successes.

Explore with your son or daughter all the ways that they are similar to other people in their life. Autistic children often feel very different from their peers and it's helpful to help them find common ground with others. Your child likes pizza and you like pizza. Your child likes horses and Auntie Jane also likes horses. Making these kinds of connections for your child can help them feel less isolated.

Again, as uncomfortable as this will be, you will need to have a look at whether you are doing anything to damage your child's self-esteem. Comparing them to other, non-autistic children, punishing them for things they cannot control (for example, having a meltdown) and talking in front of them about what a difficult time you are having in sorting things out on their behalf are all very damaging.

Help your child to understand themselves

Shortly after I began to identify as autistic, it occurred to me that I had no idea who I really was. I was in my early 40s, had worked in marketing for 20ish years, had relationships, marriages, friendships, and so on. However, looking back on my life I could see that I had fallen or ricocheted into almost everything I had ever done, like a pinball bouncing around inside someone else's game. This was an unsettling realization.

I had spent so much of my life masking and being what other people wanted me to be that I didn't know what I actually enjoyed. This was disconcerting and made me feel empty and sad. What were *my* interests? What food do *I* like to eat? This set off a long and interesting voyage of discovery into what those things were. Although it was fun to try new things and work out what fit and what didn't, I wished I could have done that decades before. This would have saved a lot of time and heartache.

You can help your child enormously by helping them to work out who they are. As I mentioned earlier about masking, autistic individuals are prone to chameleoning their way through life, morphing into their surroundings but never being truly themselves. It takes conscious effort for an autistic person to stop and listen to their true inner voice about what they actually like doing, where they like going, what feels right to them, and so on.

Helping your child to understand themselves is incredibly valuable. This is not as daunting a task as it sounds, and it is a wonderful way for you to get to know your child while helping them explore life from an internal and external perspective.

Talk to your child about their favourite things. This may take a lot of discussion as it's likely your child doesn't know what their favourite things are. By helping them to look at what they actually like to do you can help them make good choices in the future. This is not only about what they like to do but what food they like, scents, places, clothing, and so on. Do they like sweet things or savoury foods? What is their favourite scent? What kinds of places do they like to go? Do they prefer the ocean or the forest? Relaxing or physical activities? What kind of people do they like to be with? By helping them to discover these things you will help them to embrace their own uniqueness and also seek out things they like. Help them to work out if they like quiet things or loud things. Dogs or cats? Painting or cooking or both? Techy things or more simple things? Understanding all these things is helpful for your child.

It is just as important for your child to understand what they don't like. Along with this, you must teach them that it is OK to say 'no' even when everyone else around them wants to do a certain thing, eat a certain food or go to a certain place that your child does not like. This is powerful stuff; teaching your child to speak up for themselves is crucial as they will need to self-advocate in a great number of different situations throughout their life. It will help them resist peer pressure, as well. A child who feels they can't say 'no' will become an adult who can't say 'no'. It's vital that we teach our children to stand up for what's right for themselves.

Make it abundantly clear to your child that what they like is OK, even if it's different to what their friends, you, or anyone else likes. Autistic individuals can sometimes have difficulty understanding that other people think differently to them. Autistic children especially struggle with this as they haven't yet gained the life skills to navigate around it. Similarly, they may not understand that it's fine to think differently to other people. We have to teach our children to think for themselves and be themselves, and that who they are is wonderful.

Discuss ethics and morals with your child. What do they believe in – about the world, people around them, what is right and wrong? Encourage your child to stand up for their beliefs. Is there a cause you could get involved with together? This could be a great way for your child to learn the importance of expressing their beliefs.

Help your child avoid (or recover from) perfectionism

Perfectionism is a pervasive and life limiting condition. It is unfortunately very common for autistic individuals to struggle with perfectionism. We can fall into the trap of believing that if our appearance, actions, work, and so on appear flawless then we can't be criticized. Feeding into this is also the belief that looking 'perfect' will help us to look more 'normal'.

Perfectionism is enormously time-consuming and stressful and takes a lot of effort to pull off. For children who lack emotional regulation skills, it can cause a great deal of anxiety. If a child believes that they must be perfect to simply leave the house, their life will be filled with anxiety.

Helping your child to recover from perfectionism is not a small job. It will take time, and as perfectionism is often a deeply ingrained habit, it can be tough to crack. Start by teaching your child that it can be better to get something done it for it to be perfect. Autistic individuals are very efficient, so anything that helps to streamline a process will be appealing.

Does your child have a favourite athlete, author, artist or musician? Explain that every person that does something well started off not knowing how to do it and making lots of mistakes. Their favourite artist will have at first just made scratches on paper, and the famous skateboarder will have fallen off their board hundreds of times.

Talk about your own mistakes and times when you were not 'perfect'. Discuss with them how you dealt with these situations and what you learned. It's important for our children to learn that good is good enough; they don't have to be perfect to be lovable and accepted.

It can also be useful to model being average. For example, my daughter and I draw together every day. During this time, I don't create masterpieces; I just do basic drawings and colour them in imperfectly. I even make a bit of a fuss if I make a mistake to show that grown-ups make mistakes, too, and we can just carry on because it's no big deal.

Help your child to set realistic goals. Sometimes children put enormous pressure on themselves to be the best at something which isn't possible given their skill set, the time they've set for it or the resources they have to hand. Help them make more down to earth plans that they will have a greater likelihood of achieving. Tread carefully here; you want to be the voice of reason while also encouraging them to try new things and aim high.

Help your child to avoid people pleasing

People pleasing is best friends with perfectionism. Just as an autistic child may need things to be perfect in order to feel 'acceptable', they may also engage in doing just about anything to please the people around them, both children and adults. As children grow into teenagers, the risks of people pleasing become greater and potentially dangerous.

Teach your child that it's OK to not be liked by everyone. Talk about situations in your life where this has happened. This is part of the process of helping your child to understand themselves and what they like and don't like. Petra told me how her daughter played Minecraft with a boy from school. She liked the boy but didn't actually enjoy playing Minecraft, so Petra helped her work out other things her daughter and the boy could do together. Your child needs to understand that they don't have to do anything they don't like, or that feels bad to them, to be liked by anyone, Grandma included.

Help your child to develop confidence in their own decisions and teach them that it's OK to say no. Teach them what I've taught you, that what other people think of them is none of their business.

Avoid constant correction

If your child needs help in a lot of areas, be especially mindful that your interaction with them does not become a constant loop of criticism. 'Tuck your shirt in', 'use your words', 'use your fork', 'lower your voice', and so on are sometimes said unconsciously by a well-meaning parent. However, think of how many critical messages you are saying to your child over the course of a day. Multiply that by weeks, months and years. Critical comments add up and this has a big impact on the self-esteem of a child who has come to believe they can't get anything right. It takes a long time for an autistic child to get to grips with life in general. Be patient.

HOW TO HELP YOUR CHILD GET TO KNOW THEMSELVES

The way you go about helping your child understand what makes them tick depends on their cognitive ability and willingness to engage. Here are some ideas that may help.

Have a look online for 'all about me' books or worksheets or make your own. You can use these to list your child's favourite things, foods, people and places. You can also help them to think about what they are good at, their strengths and skills, and write these in the book as well. It's worth updating this kind of thing at least once a year – perhaps at the beginning of the school or calendar year – to help your child see how they change over time.

Similarly, you can help your child create (or make for them) an 'all about me' board. Glue onto the board pictures of your child's favourite things. This can be a comforting thing to look at during times of stress.

Make a positivity jar by providing a jar with small, colourful pieces of paper that your child can write on when things go well or something nice happens. They can refer to these notes when they are having a tough time to remember that it won't last, and things will soon be OK.

You can buy 'strength cards' which have different cards for positive qualities like 'caring', 'brave', 'strong' and 'creative'. As autistic individuals are often visual learners, cards like these can help your child take in the good things about themselves in a way they may not if they were simply told them by an adult.

Help your child find their tribe

We all have a desperate need to belong; it's hard-wired into us. Humans need other humans, especially those we have something in common with. Has your child ever met another neurodivergent child or been around other autistic people? If they have never met someone else like them, it's no wonder if they feel like a stranger in a strange land.

It can be difficult to find other children for your son or daughter to connect with. However, there are a growing number of youth clubs and activity groups for children and young people with additional needs. See Chapter 4 for more information on how to find these groups.

Don't just focus on autism- or disability-related groups. Sometimes the best way to help your child make friends is by focusing on their special interests. Gaming groups, cosplay clubs, public Lego sessions or other activities can help your child connect with others who share their interests.

Many years ago, I had a terrible job organizing activities for elderly people. I had no training on how to do this and had no experience of working or even spending time with elderly people. I mistakenly thought that all the people I was supporting would like all of the things I organized. Of course, they were all as different as you and me: they all liked different things and had different interests. Similarly, it's important to take care when trying to help your child connect with others. Just because something has 'autistic' in the description doesn't mean it will be right for your child. Similarly, if your friend has an autistic child who is the same age and/or has similar interests, don't expect these two kids to automatically hit it off. Go gently here and listen to what your child says they like or don't like.

It can take a long time for autistic children to understand the value of friendship. This can be especially true of children with learning disability. Their view may be that adults can bring things to them and do things for them, but children can't, so there's no point in interacting with other children. If your child is desperate to make friends, then by all means help them to do this. However, it's crucial to note that for some autistic individuals, connecting with others is simply not that important. Have a close look at whether your child wants to make friends, or if it's just that you want this for them. It can be difficult to come to terms with the idea that your son or daughter may have no interest in other people. However, what they want and need in their lives in terms of friendships must be respected, whether or not you understand it.

Be aware, too, that your child may be connecting with a lot of people online. Online friendships are just as valid as 'real life' ones. If your child is an active gamer or otherwise connecting (in a safe way, of course) with others online, and they are happy with this level of sociability, don't push them to have in-person friendships.

Talking to your child about autism

The way you handle autism with your child is very important. Autism is an integral part of your child, and you will need to help them understand and assimilate this knowledge, just like you have had to do. I have included this information here as it feeds directly into self-esteem and supporting your child with anxiety. If you have an anxious child, helping them to understand that they are autistic and how that impacts on their life will be especially important.

When to talk to your child about autism

When you tell your child about autism is very personal. Some parents wait until their child has been given a diagnosis before talking to them about autism. It may feel awkward to talk about it before it's 'official'. However, remember that your child has needs and challenges whether they have a diagnosis or not. Your child is neurodivergent, and so this may be the angle you take if you don't feel comfortable talking about autism just yet.

There are some solid clues that will tell you when it's time to talk to your child about their neurodivergence. First, if their self-awareness reaches a point where they become cognizant of the fact that they are different to others, and it's causing them distress, talking to them about what makes them different will be a kindness. Similarly, if your child is struggling with a wide variety of things, explaining autism to them could be beneficial. However you approach it, you must talk to your child about their neurodivergence or autism before they overhear a conversation about themselves or before someone else tells them.

Some children know they are autistic long before they are told. If you have been attending events and activities for children with additional needs, they may already be aware they are different from 'typical' children. Perhaps there are autistic children at school, or they have seen something about autism on television that resonated with them. Our kids can be far more switched on than we realize.

How to talk to your child about autism

Again, this is very subjective and will depend on your child. Here are some ideas:

- Talk about the things they do or the things that cause them distress (any sensory sensitivities, social difficulties, etc.) and how they relate to autistic traits.

- Focus on their strengths – memory, detail, honesty, and so on.

- Talk about famous people with autism – Lionel Messi, Elon Musk, Melanie Sykes, Chris Packham, many others.

- Explain that the diagnosis is beneficial for their future and that it may help them get more support at school and in future employment.

- Normalize autism. It is a part of your child's life and your family's life, and just one of many things that make up who they are.

- Ensure they understand that while autism is part of them, it isn't all of them. They are still the wonderful child they were before the diagnosis.

- You may find it better to drip feed information about autism into conversations over time, than to have one 'big conversation' about your child's diagnosis. If you see an autistic character in a film, or if you have an autistic relative, these can be useful conversation starters.

Why it's important to tell your child that they are autistic

Over the years, I have heard heartbreaking stories of adults who were diagnosed as autistic when they were children but were never told. These people had challenging lives, always feeling different to the rest of the world but never understanding why. At some point they learned the truth, but often after decades of struggle.

This is why it is vital for you to tell your child that they are autistic. They may feel so different to the rest of the world that understanding they are autistic may help them to find their place. Learning about their diagnosis may lead to them researching the condition to learn more, through books, videos and other means to feel more at ease about it. The earlier they learn about their diagnosis and how to talk about their needs and ask for reasonable accommodations the better, as it will help them in the future.

Our children need to understand that they are capable, clever, functioning, contributing and important members of society. Understanding that they are autistic will help them as they get older to find their place in the world; the autism community is a supportive tribe. Learning about their diagnosis, especially if your child is one who masks to fit in, can be life-changing in a positive way.

CHAPTER 14

Emotional Regulation

Emotional regulation is a skill you will need to teach your child. It takes a great deal longer for autistic children to learn how to regulate their emotions than it does for non-autistic children. Once again, I ask you to be patient. Practice and perseverance are the keys to success.

Meltdowns, shutdowns and tantrums

There are three ways an autistic person expresses distress: meltdowns, shutdowns or tantrums. It's important to understand the differences between these.

A meltdown is caused when a person becomes totally overwhelmed by sensory stimulation and/or emotions. It may be caused by sudden overload or it may be the result of many things building up over time. For example, a person may have a meltdown if:

- they witness an accident where there is a lot of noise and emotional upset, or

- they didn't sleep well, their favourite breakfast was unavailable, a sibling broke one of their toys, they were unable to complete a usual ritual or routine, and they have a painful ingrowing toenail that their parent isn't yet aware of. All of these things add up to an overloaded child that may have a meltdown.

A person who is having a meltdown is out of control of their actions. You must never punish your child when they have a meltdown.

Remember: your child is not giving you a hard time; your child is having a hard time.

Meltdowns can happen anytime. With experience, you may be able to pick up on when your child is heading for a meltdown, and you will learn how best to support them. Meltdowns aren't interested in your schedule or getting to the cinema on time. They must be allowed to run their course.

How to support your child during a meltdown

When a child has a meltdown, the parent's first instinct is to help them. It's crucial to remember that when your child is having a meltdown, they are already overloaded.

Meltdowns at home

When your child has a meltdown at home you must do all you can to keep everyone present as safe as possible. Some children cannot be alone when they are having a meltdown. This can be very difficult as they may be physically aggressive or violent when they are distressed. If this is the case, do your best to protect yourself as you help them to calm down. If it is possible to safely put your child in a room by themselves, do so, provided they are safe there. Also:

- reduce sensory stimuli

- remove extra people

- stop talking, even if you feel the need to say reassuring things; this can add to sensory overload

- remember that your child is out of control and desperate to regain control and get back to a calm place

- wait it out

- understand they may not remember what they did

- they may feel great remorse if they have hurt someone or broken something.

Meltdowns outside the home

A meltdown that happens while you are out of the house is probably one of the most stressful things you and your child will ever endure. When out of the house there is the difficulty of not always being able to keep everyone safe and you may have to deal with unhelpful strangers.

If a meltdown occurs when you are not at home, you have to become superhuman. By this I mean you must help your child by any means necessary. This may mean doing things quite dramatically out of your comfort zone like asking strangers for help, picking up your child and running to the car or taking an Uber 200 yards up a road to get home as quickly as you can. I have done all these things, so can reliably say they are possible.

Things you can do to support your child during a meltdown in public

- Remember that you do not need to explain your child's behaviour to strangers

- keep everyone as safe as possible

- remember that your child is extremely distressed and out of control

- accept that you must do everything possible to help your child

- remember what other people think of you is none of your business

- ask for help:
  - a quiet room
  - a blanket
  - help with bags
  - a reduction in sensory stimuli
  - remove extra people.

My top tip: try visualizing yourself, your child and whoever else is with you in a bubble where there's just you and the public doesn't exist. We've all heard those stories of the woman who lifted a heavy car or boat all by herself to save a child. We must be that person when our child is in distress. There is no option but to be assertive to help your child. Remember you are unlikely to ever see the person you are asking (or demanding) help from again. Their opinion of you is not important.

Just like your child may be regretful after a meltdown, you may be embarrassed by things you've said or done to help your child when they are going through one. My advice here is to let it go. You are unlikely to see whoever you shouted at again and you were doing what you absolutely had to do to help your child.

Meltdowns vs. tantrums

A meltdown occurs when the individual is so overwhelmed with emotions and/or sensory stimulation that they lose control. The person goes into a panic state, desperate to find a way to regulate what is happening inside themselves to get back to their normal base state. They may become aggressive or violent, put themselves on the ground or break things in an attempt to calm themselves.

It is easy to confuse a meltdown with a tantrum, as a child having a tantrum can also present with extreme behaviour. As autistic individuals are generally younger in themselves than their age on paper, you may see an autistic teenager having the type of tantrum you might expect from a toddler. The extreme nature of a tantrum may be entirely out of proportion to the situation.

The difference between a tantrum and a meltdown is, that with a tantrum, the child is in control and the tantrum will stop if they get what they want. For example, say a child wants chocolate. The parent says, 'no', and the child becomes aggressive and angry. If the parent gives the child the chocolate, the tantrum stops.

It's important to note that sometimes a tantrum will turn into a meltdown if the child lacks the ability to self-regulate. If the child wants something that is simply impossible that the parent can't provide, the tantrum may spiral into a meltdown where the child becomes out of control.

Do not ask your child why they are upset when they are having a meltdown. They will not be able to answer and your question may make things worse. Similarly, always remember that your child is out of control when they are having a meltdown. While thinking the situation through to determine what caused the meltdown is wise for the future, it's not appropriate to pick through what happened during this time in order to 'teach your child a lesson'.

An extremely valuable thing I have learned is that giving in to what feels like an unreasonable demand when a child is extremely upset (for example, chocolate for breakfast) is often a wise crisis aversion technique. I guarantee that if you do this, it will not cause your child to demand chocolate for breakfast every day as it will have just been what they needed to feel safe in that given situation.

What is a shutdown?

You may have heard about meltdowns, but what about shutdowns? A shutdown has the same cause – emotional or sensory overload – but presents in a very different way to a meltdown. Shutdowns can happen as a result of a period of high demand, for example exams at school or the child feeling like they have to mask in order to be accepted. Instead of lashing out as a way to self-regulate, a person having a shutdown will pull into themselves. They may:

- become nonspeaking and uncommunicative

- lose the ability to perform basic tasks, like getting dressed

- try to make themselves appear as small as possible

- need a dark, quiet place to recover

- need to lie on the floor, possibly under furniture, to regain a feeling of safety

- fall asleep because they are so overloaded.

To reiterate: both meltdowns and shutdowns must be allowed to run their course. There is no hurrying the recovery of either. Your child may recover very quickly from a meltdown or shutdown, or they may need hours or days. Respect and provide what they need to recover. Over time, you will learn what your child needs to help them recover. Some will want to be left alone and others will need a lot of reassurance and physical comfort.

Remember that while your child's meltdowns, tantrums or shutdowns may seem very extreme now, this will get better. Just as you learned emotional regulation, social and communication skills as you matured into adulthood, so will your child. They may take a bit of a winding path to get there, but they will gain self-regulation skills in time. When you go through a distressing time (for both you and your child) it's natural to feel like things will be this way forever. I promise it will get better.

HOW TO FALL IN LOVE WITH YOUR CHILD

It's easy to dwell on the challenging things you encounter with your child. However, remember that they are not their behaviour. He or she is a wonderful, funny, clever person with huge potential. They want to do well and make you proud of them.

If you are going through a difficult time with your child, instead of focusing on the negative things, look for the positives. Sometimes, the positive will be a small thing. Perhaps they put their cereal bowl in the sink without being asked, or they gave you an unexpected hug.

Grab hold of these heartening moments. Write them down in a journal, or make a gratitude jar where you can keep notes of all of the happy times for future reference. (I've called these 'golden moments' previously in this book.)

Remind yourself of what you like and love about your child. What do they do well? What are some of the great times you have had together in the past? What are some of their recent accomplishments? Simply writing these things down will warm your heart.

Most importantly, *tell your child what you love about them*. If your days have been fraught with tension and arguments, this will be distressing for your child as well. Talk to them about the things they do well. Remind them of the times when they were successful.

Your child needs to know, beyond the shadow of a doubt, that your love is unconditional and that you will be there for them no matter what happens. Don't assume they know. Tell them.

How to teach your child emotional regulation

As I've mentioned, we have to teach our autistic children everything. This includes how to manage emotions. Emotional regulation can feel like an abstract concept when you first begin to look at it. Emotional regulation is the ability to:

- recognize emotions and understand their meaning

- manage emotions to keep ourselves and others safe

- recognize and understand others' emotions

- differentiate bodily sensations from emotions and vice versa.

Does your child know which emotion is which? Many autistic children only understand very basic emotions, like happy, sad and angry. More sophisticated emotions such as disappointed, excited and jealous are more difficult to grasp. It's common for autistic people to struggle with reading facial expressions, tone of voice and body language, which adds more layers of difficulty to understanding emotions.

Some autistic individuals have a condition called alexithymia which means they struggle to feel and identify emotions. It may be difficult to separate traits of alexithymia from autistic traits. Not all autistic people have alexithymia but many autistic people do struggle with emotions.

It may be difficult for your child to differentiate between bodily sensations and emotions. Am I hungry or nervous? Am I tired or sad? Am I excited or do I need the toilet? It will take time and require support, but your child will come to understand the difference and how to manage each sensation. Being able to work out what is a body signal and what is an emotion is to do with one of our senses that is called interoception. It is well worth researching this topic to find ways to help your son or daughter unpick physical sensations from emotions.

WHAT TO DO IF YOU HAVE A CHRONICALLY ANGRY CHILD

Anger is an addictive emotion. Being angry creates a rush of adrenaline which causes physical symptoms such as a racing heart, churning stomach and sweating palms. If your child is a sensory seeker, meaning they generally seek out sensory stimulation, anger can become a problem because it is an easy way to get a big sensory hit.

If you have a chronically angry child that you suspect is creating drama by picking fights and creating other problems for themselves, you may have an anger addict on your hands. It's crucial that you work quickly to break the patterns of this destructive behaviour.

Understand that anger and upset create chemical reactions in the body that feel like sensory input which is why this behaviour is addictive and your child keeps engaging in it. Look (urgently) for ways to bring more sensory input activities into your child's life. Sensory toys, aromatherapy, colour-changing lights, resistance bands, squashing putty with their hands and listening to music are all great options.

Break the cycle of anger by changing routines. For example, if your child gets angry about a specific situation at home, explore how you can change that. Sometimes even moving furniture or changing artwork at home can help. In hope of curbing his daughter's smashing her phone against the wall and causing damage, Phillip put a large, colourful wall hanging over the damaged area. The smashing stopped immediately and was not replaced by another destructive behaviour.

Get them moving – kickboxing, weight workouts on YouTube, swimming, whatever works! As I've mentioned elsewhere, anything that uses large muscle groups is calming. Even chewing gum can be helpful as it uses powerful jaw muscles.

In time these things will help your son or daughter to self-regulate and you will hopefully be able to move them on from this behaviour to something healthier.

How to teach your child about emotions

Make learning about emotions part of daily life. Label your child's emotions and your own: happy, tired, disappointed, afraid, anxious, sad, jealous, and so on. Help your child to see that there is a broad range of emotions from 'everything is OK' to 'I'm really angry/upset'.

Discuss your own emotions with them, and model to them how you cope with these emotions to get yourself back to your contented space again. Talk about emotions at every opportunity. When watching a film or television, talk about what the characters are feeling. When talking about a work or family situation, talk about the emotions involved.

There are a lot of products available to help you teach your child about emotions. Emotion cards and games are helpful. There are some excellent books about autism and emotions. See wdisbook. com/resources for a list of these.

Teaching emotional regulation

Bear in mind that your child is just that: a child. As such they will not have the capacity for emotional regulation that an older child or adult has. Your child's emotional state is affected by many things. The environment, other people present, sensory disturbances, lack of sleep and what they have or haven't eaten all have an impact on emotions.

Emotions are not good or bad; they are neutral. It's how your child copes with emotions that matters. Ensure that your child understands that it's OK to feel whatever they feel and that it's not bad to feel big emotions. Girls especially are put under pressure by society to be 'nice' or 'good' and never get angry or sad so it's vital to make sure your daughter knows that whatever she feels is fine.

It's also important to explain to your child that even huge upsets will fade in time. Autistic individuals can sometimes feel that what is happening now is forever and so big emotions can feel especially scary. Perhaps in the past, you have had an upsetting experience or heartbreak that you felt you would never recover from, but you did. Sharing your own personal experiences of managing emotional episodes is a great way to teach your child about emotions.

Look for patterns in your child's emotions. If your son is often upset when plans fall through with his other parent, or your daughter is excited every Saturday when she goes to her youth group, these are great teaching opportunities. It's also useful for you to note, either mentally or formally, if your child's emotions can be linked to outside influences such as certain foods, people, environments, and so on.

You will need to teach your child how to appropriately respond to frustration, anger and anxiety. You are the best role model for this. Talk to your child about your own emotions and how you manage them. Autistic individuals, especially children, often think that they are the only person who feels a certain way. It's vital to help your child understand that everyone worries and gets sad, angry and upset.

Remember that feelings are very real to the person feeling them. Validate your child's feelings, even if they feel over the top to you. Be compassionate, understanding and non-judgemental. This will require a great deal of patience at times but it's crucial to let them experience and work through their feelings without fear of criticism.

HORMONES!

Hormones have a huge impact on emotions. Some autistic children tend to start puberty earlier than their non-autistic peers, so you may begin to see the effect of hormones at an earlier age than expected. At times you may feel like your family is being held hostage by your child's hormones! If you have a daughter, it might be worth keeping a diary of her emotions. Girls will experience cyclical emotional differences long before they begin to have periods. A journal will help you see patterns in her behaviour and pre-empt or prepare for the distressing feelings she may have.

It can be tempting to avoid situations that might cause upset for your child. Remember that life is a great practice ground, and that the best way for your son or daughter to learn emotional regulation is to have experiences that require it. Your child needs to develop these skills as part of growing up and gaining independence.

You may find it beneficial to introduce new situations gradually and in a way that works for your child. For example, I recently wanted to take my daughter to a new café. She loves cafés and I knew she would enjoy going to this place once she was comfortable with it. This was how I encouraged her to do this:

- First, we drove by the café a few times and I simply pointed at it and said, 'look, there's a new café'.

- For the next few visits, I pulled into the car park, paused, turned around and went home.

- For a few more visits, we went to the café, parked up, got out of the car, went to the door and looked inside.

- Finally, we were able to go into the café and have cake.

Managing new situations in this way takes time and patience but can reap great rewards and help your child access new places and activities. Candice wanted to introduce her daughter to a new sensory centre in town. She went about this in a similar way as I did with the café, driving to the place, having a look around outside, and so on. She found she was able to book a private session for her daughter so that she could see what it was like with no one in it. What a great idea!

Focus on the positives

Negativity breeds negativity. If you know that your child is focused on the negative things in their life, it's important that you help them shift their mindset. In every person's day, there are negative and positive experiences. Help your child find the good things in each day, even if they are small, such as seeing a friend at school or eating a favourite food.

It can be helpful to end the day with a 'gratitude roundup' where you and your child each name three good things that have happened during the day. Over time, the positive experiences may add up and overshadow the negative things.

Provide the safest place

I hate to break it to you, but your child's behaviour will be at its worst when they are with you. This may make you feel that your child does not like you or is seeking out ways to cause upset. The exact opposite is true: your child knows that you will not stop loving them no matter what they do. They feel safest with you, which means they can be entirely themselves in your presence. They can do whatever is needed to bring themselves back to a calm state. The more challenging you find your child, the more distressed they are, so it's vital to find ways to help them.

Conversely, a child may be on their best behaviour in places where they feel the most unsafe. At school, with some friends and relatives and in some public settings your child may appear to have it all together. If they then come home and explode or shut down, this is a good indicator of how unsafe they feel in those situations.

What helps your child to feel safe? Is it time with Dad or a hug from Mum? Wrapping up in a duvet or weighted blanket? Reading or gaming? A walk in the park or time with a pet? Whatever it is, help your child to work out what they need so that you can help them access that when they need to. It's important for you to understand what these things are to help them calm down and recover from upset. Many autistic children need to decompress in some way after holding it together all day at school. This is not the time to ask how their day was or how they are feeling. Find out what makes them feel safe and provide that for them for as long as they need it. When they've come back to themselves, then you can ask about their day.

Find calming things you can do together, such as blowing bubbles, baking, jigsaw puzzles or crafts. These can take your child's mind off their worries and help them to relax. By helping your child to work out what helps them to feel secure, you will provide them with the tools to do this for themselves in the future.

THE EMPATHY MYTH

There is a common belief that autistic people lack empathy. This is founded on the fact that sometimes autistic people don't react when sad or upsetting things happen to themselves or others. The reality is that this happens not because of a lack of empathy but too much empathy.

When sad or distressing things happen, for example, the death of a pet, this can be overwhelming for an autistic individual. Instead of responding in a way society deems appropriate, such as crying and appearing sad, some autistic people emotionally shut down. They may appear completely unaffected by what has happened. This is also true if something bad happens to a friend or relative.

What's really happening is an internal damage limitation exercise. In essence, the autistic person puts the upsetting situation into a mental compartment to stop it from overwhelming them. It may never come out of this compartment, or it may come out much later. You may have a child who is so upset by the death of a grandparent that they lock the emotions around this away for years and will suddenly begin to talk about it long after the fact.

I have had this experience many times in my own life. The number of sympathy cards I've bought but never sent attests to this. Extreme emotion, whether my own or someone else's, is often too much for me to cope with. The exercise of locking the emotion away is tangible; it's something I choose to do for self-preservation. These days, therapy helps me work through these feelings in real time.

It's difficult as a parent not to be upset by what appears to be a cold, uncaring attitude from your child. Rest assured that your child has felt whatever's happened very deeply, whether or not they give any indication of this.

The importance of movement

Provide your son or daughter with every opportunity to move, especially engaging in activities that use major muscle groups. We know it can be difficult to motivate some children to get exercise, but you may be able to encourage movement through chores, walking the dog or calming activities like yoga or trampolining.

Tips for getting your child moving

If your child is very anxious, they will want to feel better. Helping them to understand that physical activity will help reduce their anxiety is important. I used to be an extremely anxious person. I found that physical exercise reduced my anxiety quickly and effectively.

Here are some ideas for motivating your child to get physical:

Focus on what they enjoy

If your child likes swimming, walking or cycling, ensure this is part of their daily routine as often as possible. It's easy to forget to do this but it's vital to help your child feel more balanced and calmer. A walk doesn't have to be a ten-mile trek. Walking the dog around the neighbourhood or finding puddles to splash in on a rainy day are equally good.

Make it a game

One great way to get your child out and about is to take part in treasure hunt activities such as Pokémon GO or Geocaching. Both involve using GPS coordinates to find characters or objects, and by default require a fair amount of walking. I've found making up games to get my daughter moving has been very successful. For example, we bounce on exercise balls every day to a count of 100. In another game we see who can move a set of weighted balls from one end of our living room to the other the fastest. These have become fun things we do together and not a push to exercise.

Little and often

Autistic people tend to be a bit 'all or nothing'. It's important to help your child understand that a bit of movement is good. Chores are a great way to get in a few bursts of movement. Taking out the rubbish, making beds, hanging up washing and carrying things up and down stairs all work.

Home workouts

Some autistic children go through phases where they do not want to go out of the house. Try video games like Just Dance, golf or tennis. YouTube has a lot of short workout options, stretching and yoga videos. A mini trampoline inside or a larger one outside can make a huge difference for an anxious child or one with energy to burn.

Make it a habit

A body in motion stays in motion. Once your child begins to realize that the simple activities they are taking part in are making a difference to their anxiety, it will be important to make these a habit. Encourage them to have a bounce on the trampoline immediately after school or do yoga before bed. Attaching exercise to another activity will help ingrain good movement habits. For example, wake up and then do a 15-minute YouTube weight workout, or come home from school and then walk the dog.

Lead by example

As with so many things, you are the best role model for exercise. You can't expect to encourage your child to exercise while you are sitting on the sofa. Without putting any effort in, I got my daughter exercising simply by doing it myself. If I watch a yoga video, she will join in. She watches me use our stationary bicycle and then she'll have a go herself. Exercise and talk about how it helps you to feel calm and grounded.

As I said at the beginning of this book, I am providing a whole new set of tools for you to put in your toolbox. Some of these strategies will work for your child and some may have left you shaking your head. If you have an anxious child, please spend some additional time with this chapter. Read it again and make notes of what you can try to help your child.

CHAPTER 15

Sensory Processing Differences

Sensory processing issues are one of the biggest causes of distress for autistic individuals. When a non-autistic person experiences sensory stimuli, the brain processes that information and automatically decides whether to filter it out or pay attention to it. Some autistic people lack this filter and so may become overloaded as the various stimuli causes a traffic jam in the brain. We also have sensitivities to things that non-autistic people don't have, and it's sometimes hard for the people around us to understand why we are so distressed.

For example, I have supersonic hearing. When I am at my partner's house, I can hear the faintest hum when his neighbour's boiler switches on at five o'clock in the morning. This wakes me up and keeps me awake, but I know that this would not bother most other people.

So many senses

We all know about the main five senses of hearing, smell, taste, touch and vision. There are several senses beyond these that are very important to learn about to understand what is going on for your child. Some scientists say there are up to 33 senses! We will just focus on the ten that most impact on autistic individuals. Beyond the main five senses, the following additional senses are important to understand:

- *The vestibular sense* deals with balance and body control, the speed the body is moving, head position, and so on.

- *The proprioceptive sense* informs the brain of where the body is in space and where it is in relation to other objects (spatial awareness).

- *The interoceptive sense* sends signals to the brain about hunger, thirst, when to use the toilet, tiredness, being too hot or too cold.

- *The thermoceptive sense* gives us the ability to sense temperature on the skin.

- *The nociceptive sense* helps us to recognize pain and respond appropriately.

Please note that I am not an occupational therapist or in any way an expert on sensory issues. As with everything in this book, I share the following for information purposes only. I feel it's important to tell you about these things as many parents who are new to autism are baffled by their child's behaviour, and if you are feeling this way, it's likely you'll find some clues in this chapter. The distress caused by sensory differences can result in anxiety and may cause a child to behave in challenging ways. If you are going through a phase of difficult behaviour with your child, have a read through the following as you may find some clues to what is causing the behaviour and come to understand that it's not the child's fault or choice, but their way of coping with sensory distress.

Sensory seekers (hyposensitive) and sensory avoiders (hypersensitive)

There are two types of people when it comes to senses. Generally, a person is either a sensory seeker or a sensory avoider. However, there may be crossovers in some areas. You probably know which of these your child is. A sensory avoider is a child who is generally hypersensitive, or over-responsive, to sensory stimuli and so seeks out quiet and low-input situations, plain surroundings, bland food, slow movement. A sensory seeker is a child who is hyposensitive, or under-responsive, to sensory stimuli and so seeks out noise, vibration, spicy food, deep pressure and big movement.

What sensory processing differences look like in day-to-day life

I want to help you get a better understanding of how each of the senses impacts on your child. I have included information about oversensitivities and undersensitivities, and ways you can support your child with each. I hope this will help you to understand your child (and perhaps yourself, or your partner) better.

The sense of hearing
Oversensitive

A person who is oversensitive to sound cannot cope in busy environments. Loud noises may actually cause them physical pain. They may struggle to make out individual sounds or voices. This person may be able to hear the tiniest bit of noise, and may have difficulty sleeping if *any* sound is present (like me with the boiler noise). They may also make repetitive noises or need to listen to music or white noise to block out unpleasant sounds.

Supports: ear defenders, ear plugs, listening to music through headphones, noise cancelling headphones, white noise (there are apps and machines to provide this).

Undersensitive

This is a person who seeks out noise! They will play music, the piano, games or the television too loudly, all of the time. They may shout or talk too loudly and are generally noisy individuals. This is the person who can sleep through anything and may even prefer to have a radio or fan on to help them sleep.

Supports: you will need to teach your child about acceptable volume levels for their voice and their activities. Something like The Incredible 5 Point Scale I mentioned earlier (easily found online) can help with this to teach your child this concept. Find ways to feed their noise craving that doesn't upset the rest of the family, for example, a fan in their bedroom and using headphones when gaming and listening to music. You will also need to take care that your child looks after their hearing as they may not understand that listening to things at high volume may cause damage.

Children who are under- or oversensitive to sound may be thought to have a hearing impairment, and your GP or health visitor may recommend a hearing test (or several) to rule this out. It's useful to have these tests done, but it is the rare autistic child who has a hearing issue. It's more often a wiring problem that causes the hyper- or hyposensitivity.

The sense of sight

Oversensitive

The individual who is oversensitive to visual stimuli will struggle with bright lights and busy environments. Where do we most find bright lights and busy environments during childhood? School, that's where! Schools are notorious for filling the walls with displays of current topics and children's work. They may even hang things from the ceiling. The classroom may have bright fluorescent lights on even on a bright, sunny day.

Supports: If you suspect your child is oversensitive in this area, you will want to be sure that your home is as neutral as possible. Busy wallpaper or patterns on furniture may cause distress for this child. Ensure that their bedroom is a calm and neutral place without a lot of bright colours or patterns. Speak to the school about any reasonable adjustments that can be made around reducing visual stimuli in the classroom.

Undersensitive

This person loves colourful lights (I am this person!). They will be drawn towards light up toys and high-action games and videos. They will like a lot of visual stimuli such as glitter lamps and busy artwork.

Supports: provide opportunities for them to feed their need for visual stimulation. Let them choose what patterns and colours they might like in their room. My daughter and I are both visual sensory seekers. Our home is full of star projectors, glitter and lava lamps, fairy lights, colourful Indian tapestries, and so on.

The sense of smell
Oversensitive
Many autistic children prefer a limited and rigid diet. This is not a behavioural problem, although it may frustrate you. The child that is oversensitive to smells may simply be unable to cope with food smells and find them nauseating. This person may also find it difficult to be around strong fragrances, such as perfumes and strongly scented washing powders or other cleaning products. They may wear the same clothing for long periods because their own smell is comforting. I have found that this issue affects me far more as I have gotten older than it did when I was a child. I can no longer tolerate any kind of fragrance in washing powder or dishwasher tablets. Sensory issues can change over time.

Supports: reduce scents at home. Choose fragrance-free cleaning products and personal care products like shampoo and soap. Be mindful of your child's needs when out and about. For example, going to a curry restaurant where the smell of the food will be very strong may not be wise. If your child is especially sensitive, you will need to speak to the people they see regularly, such as relatives and teachers, about avoiding fragrances when around your child.

Undersensitive
This is the child who cannot smell what you smell. A young autistic child with this undersensitivity may mouth and lick objects to work out what they are as they cannot get the scent of the item. It's not that they can't smell, it's just that they smell things differently to others. They may not smell warning smells like smoke or chemicals, or when food has gone bad.

Supports: talk about other ways to interpret warning signs, like seeing smoke or spots of mould. Talk to your child about how to tell what something is made of by touching it. Help them to compensate for their undersensitive sense of smell by using their other senses.

The sense of taste
Oversensitive
The child who is oversensitive to taste prefers bland foods. They may gag on food (this is also linked to touch oversensitivity). They may not eat even when hungry because they are worried about something being too strongly flavoured.

Supports: don't fight this. Do not force your child to try new foods if they have this oversensitivity. Provide the foods that they will eat. I know this is scary. To get additional nutrients into them, try fortified milkshakes or a flavourless vitamin powder. My daughter eats an entirely beige diet of porridge, toast, pasta and chicken nuggets. Fortunately, she will take supplements to top up what she's missing.

Undersensitive
This child may chew non-food items like cardboard or clothing. (Note: this may be confused with the condition Pica, where a person eats non-food items. The undersensitive child doesn't eat non-food things; they just like to chew them.) They may also lick objects. The individual who is undersensitive to taste may crave crunchy, textured and spicy foods.

Supports: provide chewing devices like chew necklaces or toys. Make high impact foods available such as rice cakes and carrot sticks. If it's safe for them to do so, try chewing gum as this provides a sensory hit and is also very calming.

The vestibular sense
Oversensitive
This individual has difficulty with balance. They may avoid stairs, swings and slides for fear of falling. The child with an oversensitive vestibular sense will dislike spinning and movement and may have a fear of their feet leaving the ground.

Supports: try gentle resistance and weightlifting exercises such as using resistance bands, rolling weighted balls and swimming. Search the internet to find core strength exercises for kids. It will help your child to feel more secure. Bouncing (not jumping) on a trampoline can also help. I bought a set of heavy plastic 'stepping stones' and I use them to make a trail across our living room floor, interspersing the stones with pillows and wobble cushions to create a gentle balance trail for my daughter, who has an oversensitive vestibular sense.

Undersensitive

The child with the undersensitive vestibular sense seeks out movement, swinging and climbing. They crave big vestibular input so may be in constant motion, seeking out ways to feed the craving.

Supports: provide deep pressure activities such as squashing them under sofa cushions or rolling them up like a sausage in a duvet, then pressing down from their head to their feet. Swimming is also a great activity for this category as it uses a lot of muscles. A trampoline is useful here. If possible, provide outdoor or indoor climbing equipment like swings and pull-up bars.

The proprioceptive sense

Oversensitive

An oversensitive proprioceptive sense creates difficulty with holding objects, such as cutlery or writing utensils. The person with this undersensitivity may have poor fine motor skills. They may have difficulty chewing. The child in this category may be afraid of running into things and avoid activities that may involve any sort of rough and tumble play. (Note: this oversensitivity can be confused with Dyspraxia, which also involves poor motor skills and clumsiness.)

Supports: you can buy specialist cutlery and pencil grips to help your child with eating and writing. Have your child engage in simple activities that feel safe to them. For example, hoovering, sweeping the floor, carrying things from one room to another may help your child get to know their body better simply by moving it. A weighted vest or rucksack may help as well. You could put wrist weights, a weighted ball or even tins of beans in your child's school bag to help with this.

Undersensitive

This area of sensory sensitivity can cause a lot of misunderstanding. The person struggles to know where their body is in space. Some individuals in this category hold their bodies in unusual postures and may have a distinctive walk. For example, some autistic children have a 'stompy' walk or they may walk on tiptoe so they can get a good proprioceptive sensory hit. The child with an undersensitive proprioceptive sense may lean against things or people, may crash into walls, furniture and people (including younger siblings) and may hit, kick, pinch or bite in order to meet their proprioceptive needs. This can easily be misunderstood as 'bad behaviour'. This child may also write heavily, tearing the paper with their pencil or pen. They may also hyperextend their joints when stretching.

Supports: see the suggestions for children with an undersensitive vestibular sense.

The interoceptive sense

Oversensitive

This person enjoys feeling bodily sensations such as hunger, thirst or the need to urinate, so they may put off doing these things. They may also like the fast breathing and increased heart rate that comes from exercise.

Supports: teach your child to eat, drink and use the toilet at specific times so that they do these things even when normally it wouldn't occur to them. This is very important: your child will struggle to gain independence if they do not know when to eat or drink, and this could cause health problems down the line.

Undersensitive

The child with an undersensitive interoceptive sense may not know when they are hungry or thirsty, but may eat or drink more than they should. They may not be able to tell if they are hot or cold, even if they are uncomfortable. This person may go to the toilet often; they can't sense when they need to go, so they take frequent loo breaks 'just in case'.

Supports: the advice here is very similar to that given for interoceptive oversensitivity. Help your child to understand when they should be eating and drinking and what standard serving sizes are. Teach them to use the toilet at set times throughout the day to avoid accidents.

The thermoceptive sense

Oversensitive

The person with thermoceptive oversensitivity will avoid heat sources. They may not like wearing clothing or coats and may complain of being too hot or too cold in mild weather. They may prefer cold foods and drinks.

Supports: ensure that your child does not get too hot. Keep them as cool as possible in hot weather by dressing them in lighter clothing, encouraging them to drink water and using fans and cooling sprays. Be mindful of putting them in too many layers in the cooler months.

Undersensitive

The child in this category will seek out cold or heat, for example putting their hands against a radiator. They like hot baths and hot food and drinks. They may wear many layers of clothing in order to feel hot.

Supports: teach your child the dangers of touching hot surfaces. It may be very tricky to stop your child wearing a coat or too many clothes in the summer and it may be a losing battle that's not worth fighting. Ensure that they stay hydrated as much as you can.

The nociceptive sense

Oversensitive

An oversensitive nociceptive sense may cause the individual to feel pain at the slightest knock. This may cause them to avoid any physical activities for fear of getting hurt.

Supports: see the suggestions for proprioceptive oversensitivity. These will also be beneficial for the child with nociceptive oversensitivity in that they may give the child physical confidence so that they will not worry so much.

Undersensitive

Nociceptive undersensitivity is very serious. A person in this category may injure themselves but have no idea that they have done it. I have heard countless stories of children who had nasty falls that weren't taken seriously by medical professionals because the child didn't cry or indicate that they were in pain. An autistic colleague of mine broke his foot in several places but didn't realize for over a week because he simply didn't feel it. This of course makes the injury much worse.

Supports: if your child is in this category, you will need to become very aware of what pain looks like for them. If they do not cry or talk about the pain, keep an eye out for swelling or if they struggle to walk or use an arm or hand. If your child is injured and you have been present, be sure to tell the medical professional you see exactly what happened and that your child is unable to feel pain. Impress upon them the importance of not taking your child's lack of reaction as a sign that nothing is wrong.

What is stimming?

'Stimming' is self-stimulatory behaviour used by individuals with autism as a way to calm themselves, self-regulate, protect themselves from overstimulation and reduce anxiety. Most stims are harmless but some may require intervention to keep the stimming person safe. There are three types of stims:

- *Hand stims:* playing with or pulling hair, picking at fingernails, flapping hands, clapping, thumb sucking, snapping fingers, pulling at (or out) eyebrows or eyelashes.

- *Body stims:* rocking, head bobbing or banging, spinning.

- *Vocal stims:* repeating words, screeching, groaning.

In my experience, stimming is something that many parents find difficult to accept and understand. A child's stims may be the one thing that visibly sets them apart as autistic. Many parents worry that this will cause problems for the child in life, in public, at school, and so on. I've been asked countless times, 'how do I get my child to stop flapping/screeching/playing with a bit of fabric?' The answer is: you don't. Stimming is necessary. It is a self-regulation tool. You never want to stop your child from stimming unless the stim is dangerous or causing physical harm.

Will a stim mark your child out as different? Of course. Your child *is* different. Stimming may cause people to stare at your child in public and children to tease them at school. This does not make it a less important activity. Your child will make their own choices about stimming. As they grow older and become more self-aware and able to self-regulate, their stims will change. They may go from flapping to stretching, or from wringing their hands to squeezing a stress ball or putty. It has to be their choice. You cannot control this.

Stims are different from tics. A tic is repetitive, uncontrollable and compulsive, whereas a stim is a chosen, generally pleasurable activity. It can be difficult to tell them apart, but if you feel that the activity is causing rather than reducing stress for your child, it's more likely to be a tic. Tics are harmless but may be uncomfortable. If your child has had repetitive tics for over a year, this may be an indication that they have Tourette's Syndrome.

Dealing with self-harm

With autistic children, there are two types of self-harm. Sometimes children engage in stims that cause bodily injury. This could be in response to stress. For example, when we moved house when my daughter was about two years old, she went through a long and difficult phase of pulling her hair out. Other children do things like pick at fingernails or skin, or lick their lips excessively, to the point where they are cracked and bleeding. Some children engage in this kind of behaviour because they like the feel of it. If you have a child who is generally undersensitive, they will need bigger hits of stimuli in order to feel things. So you may have a child who is injuring themselves in some way because they crave sensory input.

The other type of self-harm is psychological. The child is so distressed that they injure themselves in order to feel something different to their emotional pain. They may cut or burn themselves or stop eating.

Whatever the cause, self-injurious behaviour must be dealt with straight away, before it becomes habitual. One way you can help your child stop this kind of behaviour is to disrupt routines. If your child is self-harming at specific times, if it is possible, change their routine to stop the habit of self-harming. For example, putting something bitter on a child's fingernails to stop them biting them to the point of drawing blood. You may also be able to distract your child from the behaviour with other stimulating options such as a massage ball or other tactile play. You could try replacing the behaviour with a slightly less damaging one. For example, giving them an elastic band to snap against their wrist or a stiff scrub brush to use on their arms and legs. Be approachable for your child. Don't make your child feel shame about this behaviour. Create an open space to talk about feelings that may be driving self-harming behaviour.

I realize that the ideas I've given above may be far too simplistic for your situation, and I am in no way making light of the seriousness of self-harm. If your child is engaging in self-harm that you are not able to help them with, please seek professional help for them.

Sensory overload

Overload can happen all at once or it can be something that builds up over time until the person is overwhelmed. Remember how I mentioned the traffic jam analogy earlier, where all the sensory stimuli build up in the brain because the person is unable to filter them. Overload will generally lead to a meltdown or shutdown. A meltdown may cause your child to behave in an aggressive or even violent way. You will need to learn to read the signs of overload in your child to help them stay regulated and calm.

Perhaps you've experienced a situation where you were so angry you wanted to respond to the situation with physical aggression. You most likely didn't do that. Instead, you went for a walk, went to the gym, talked to a friend, or did something else to cool off. Similarly, you must help your child to manage their emotions and sensory processing differences in more healthy ways. Over time, you will learn to read the signs that your child is moving towards overload. That is the time to reduce sensory stimuli – turn off lights and music, reduce the number of people around them and direct them towards calming activities.

Sensory input and sensory reduction activities and equipment

Sensory input or stimuli include anything that engages the senses. It's worth investing in a good book or two about autism and the senses to help you understand your child's needs. You can use sensory stimulation or reduction to avoid distress and in turn reduce the challenging behaviour that might be a result of that distress. For example, if you have a child who is constantly chewing the collars and cuffs of their school shirts or chewing non-food items, a chewy device can help with this. There are many options with these; some are very inconspicuous like grey dog tags, beaded necklaces or cuff bracelets. A trampoline might help with the child who is crashing into furniture (or siblings!) because they are seeking deep sensory input. Swimming uses all the major muscle groups so is very calming. Fiddle toys may curb boredom which can lead to distress. The internet is full of sensory activities.

Sensory toys and devices are like wedding cakes. If you go into a shop to buy a 'cake' it costs £10, but if you go into the same shop to buy the same cake but it's now called a 'wedding cake', it will cost £100. Sensory toys are no different. You can go into a discount shop and buy a balance cushion for £4.99 or you can order a 'disability wobble cushion' for £36. You do not need to spend a lot of money on sensory toys and devices. Another example: you could buy a specialist autism blackout tent for £180 or you could go into a sporting goods shop and buy a one man pop-up tent for £35. The pop-up tent may not entirely cut out light, but it will create a safe space for your child, away from everyone else, and serve the same purpose as the blackout tent.

It's important to create a sensory diet for your child. A sensory diet isn't about food but about a range of activities you can have your child engage in each day to help them, and help to teach them, to self-regulate. Some examples include a session of sensory play, where they are digging toys out of a box of rice, having their skin brushed with a sensory brush or walking on different textures of fabric. What will work for your child may take a bit of trial and error but it's worth the effort. I've included more information about sensory diets at wdisbook.com/resources.

Sensory issues and autism is a vast subject, and I am barely scratching the surface here. I urge you to do further research on this so that you have a deeper understanding of your child's sensory needs. As sensory over- or undersensitivities can cause a lot of distress, it's worth taking a lot of time to learn more and investigate what works for your child. Be patient with this as it will take time, but the payoff will be worth it.

CHAPTER 16

Communication

Many autistic individuals struggle with communicating their thoughts, wants and needs. It's common for autistic people to misread or misunderstand social cues, body language, facial expressions and tone of voice. We have difficulty interacting with others and knowing when to speak up or respond and when to stay quiet. Even the simplest social interactions can be fraught with complexity.

The point of this chapter is to help you understand that, for autistic individuals, communication is not at all straightforward. Speaking, understanding, making sense of tone of voice and body language take time and are not easy things to learn. This is a short chapter simply because this is not my area of expertise and it also requires more technical information than is appropriate for the scope of this book. I have included a range of communication resources at wdisbook.com/resources that may be useful to you.

Behaviour is communication

Your child may pull you towards what they want, point, repeat phrases from their favourite show, cry or act aggressively to communicate with you. It's important to see that all of these things are ways your child tells you what they want and need and what is happening for them.

Extra processing time

Many autistic children need extra time to process what has been said to them. Some people call this the 'eight second rule', where you give a child eight seconds to respond before repeating what you've said. Some children need far more time, like 20 seconds. It's useful to understand this about your child as otherwise you may think they are not listening or ignoring you. If this is the case, try giving them a bit of extra time, repeating the request or question and see what happens. With my daughter, I will ask something (for example, 'please close the curtains') and actually wait a minute or two before asking again. Sometimes I have to ask three or four times, but the request is met eventually.

Speech delay

Some autistic children have delayed speech. If your child is non-speaking, you will be desperate to help them speak and to know when they will speak. There is no easy answer or solution here. I will say that people begin speaking at all different ages. I know of a young man who was nonspeaking until he was 21 and now talks constantly. Please do not worry if your child is not yet speaking. They will find their way with a communication method that works for them. At 13, my daughter's communication (she did not speak until she was four-and-a-half) is limited, but she can get her basic needs met and communicate some more complex observations and information.

It's important to note that nonspeaking doesn't mean not intelligent. It may be difficult to understand or accept in a world that places such high value on spoken communication. Your child is a beautiful, funny, wonderful person whether they speak or not. It may be that they will communicate with a sign language, such as Makaton or other sign language. They may use picture communication, like PECS or other visuals. There are also apps and devices that support speech, like ProLoQuo and GoTalk. Try different things to find what works for them.

HOW TO SUPPORT NONSPEAKING CHILDREN

You can use a variety of tools to help your nonspeaking child to communicate. Speech is an extremely complicated thing for the brain to master. Helping your child to get their needs met while they are developing speech will reduce stress and anxiety for them and you.

Picture Exchange Communication (PECS)

You can teach your child how to request the things he or she wants and needs by using pictures. For example, your child gives you a picture of a drink, and you give them the drink. There is a lot of information online about how to use PECS, and formal training from the creators of PECS, Pyramid Education Consultants. The training is very good and worth doing.

Communication apps and AT/AAC devices

Over the past decade, the number of communication apps and assistive technology (AT) and alternative and arranged communication (AAC) devices has grown dramatically. There are dozens of apps you can try with your child. Just skimming through Apple's AppStore, I find Grid-Player, Visuals2Go, Vocable AAC, TouchChat and many more. There are also several options on the device front, some of which may be available via the NHS. What works for my child may not work for yours, so you will want to try different apps to see what works best.

Visual tools

Using visuals like those covered in Chapter 12 are incredibly helpful for nonspeaking children. Visual schedules, now and next boards and social stories can all help you to communicate with your child and help them understand what is going on.

Label everything

Whenever you are with your child, actively verbally label everything you both touch. 'Teddy', 'cup', 'crayon', 'dolly', 'blocks'. You will get into the habit of doing this (and may find yourself doing it even when you are not with your child).

Don't force it

It's very tempting to try and encourage your child to speak by forcing them to ask for what they want. Don't do this. If your child is not speaking it is because it is impossible for them to do so for one reason or another. Forcing them to say the word 'biscuit' in order to get a biscuit is mean.

Patience, patience, patience

If you have a nonspeaking child, I truly feel your anguish. As I've said, there is no guide or way to work out when your child will speak. You just have to be very patient and work on helping them to communicate to get their needs met.

Echolalia

Echolalia is when a person repeats words or phrases over and over. Sometimes this is a sensory pleasure and the person just likes how it feels and sounds to say that word or phrase. Sometimes the person is repeating a phrase from a video or television show they have seen. If you know the show, you may be able to work out the meaning of the phrase by understanding its context. A child who uses echolalia may repeat things that are said to them. Echolalia mustn't be dismissed as meaningless babble. If your child is echolalic, pay close attention to what they are saying and when they are saying it. Upon closer inspection, you may find that they are actually communicating very clearly by repeating certain things.

Jumbled up words

Some children have an audio processing disorder, which makes it difficult for them to take in information and to replicate the words and sounds that they hear. This may also cause them to mix up the things they say. For example, my daughter has audio processing disorder and she will say 'rice cakes' when she means 'scratch my back' and vice versa. It takes intuition and patience to decode the language of a child with audio processing disorder. There is unfortunately very little support for children with audio processing disorder. I personally believe that in some cases it is a severe delay that will catch up in time.

Selective mutism

This is a condition characterized by a fear of speaking in certain situations. A child with selective mutism may have such extreme anxiety around certain people or in certain places (for example, school) that they cannot speak. Some children with selective mutism may be able to speak or whisper to certain 'safe' people. Selective mutism can be very confusing to parents as it may appear that the child is 'putting it on' if they are able to speak to some people but not others. However, it is something to take seriously and treat with compassion. Please see Chapter 13 for more information about social anxiety.

Spiky speech profile

Remember how I talked about the spiky profile in Chapter 11? A child who speaks may still have difficulty expressing himself or explaining their thoughts and actions. Your child may speak very clearly and have high intelligence but still may lack the ability to communicate certain things, especially when stressed. This may be confusing and will require your patience to unpick what is going on or what has happened. It's fair to say that some autistic children lack the understanding that their parents are not psychic. We don't know what they are thinking and cannot see what they see in their minds, but it takes time for them to understand this.

Alternative communication for speaking children

Some autistic people can speak but choose not to because the effort it takes to move words from brain to mouth is just too great. Your child may prefer to speak via text, email or a communication app. If this is what is most comfortable for them, please respect it. It does not mean your child is being lazy, but that they are self-aware enough to understand that this is how they need to communicate. Some children also struggle with people looking at them while they talk, especially when they are talking about something stressful. Many parents find it best to have those more emotional conversations while sitting side by side in the car, or in the dark at bedtime.

Social skills

Autistic children learn social skills by being taught them. This takes time. Teaching your child about emotions, tone of voice and body language are all crucial here. Always remember that your child doesn't know what they don't know. For example, they may not know that crying means 'sad' or that a raised voice and scowling face means 'angry'. Therefore, they may not react appropriately to the people around them who are expressing strong feelings until they are taught how to tell what other people are feeling.

CHAPTER 17

Education

I hate to be the bearer of bad news, but at some point in your autism journey, you are going to struggle to get adequate support for your child. I wish this wasn't the case. I don't know a single parent of an autistic child who has not had to go to battle for something or other. The SEND (Special Educational Needs and Disabilities) system in the UK is very broken. This chapter will arm you with the information you need to get the support your child requires at school.

When to talk to the school about your child's needs

When your child starts at a new school or setting, or begins a new school year, you will want to speak to the school staff about your child. As I said in Chapter 5, this does not mean supplying a 12-page dossier about your child, but telling them the most important things they need to know.

It will be necessary to talk to the school about your child's needs if their behaviour at home changes, or if anxiety causes them to miss school. If staff indicate there is an issue at parents' evening, this is also a sign you need to get involved. Crucially, when your gut instinct tells you that something just isn't right, you need to act on that feeling.

Call a meeting

Worry that something isn't right at school requires decisive action. You are not at school with your child so it's vital that you go and speak to school staff about any concerns you have. Don't worry about being 'that parent'. See the information in Chapter 5 about how to be assertive with education professionals to guide you through what you need to do here.

Who to talk to about your child's needs

There are several people you can contact about getting your child adequate support at school:

- *Your child's teacher* is your first point of contact about your child. They are a very important ally in getting support.

- *The school SENCo (Special Educational Needs Co-ordinator).* Every school has a SENCo. They exist to ensure your child gets the help that they need in order to thrive at the school.

- *The headteacher* should be an approachable person with whom you can have reasonable conversations about your child's needs.

- *Parent support liaison.* Some schools will have a parent support person. This person may be a more neutral party you can discuss your child with.

- *SEN governor.* All schools are required to have a SEN governor. You will generally not speak to the SEN governor unless you cannot get help from anyone else in the school.

Applying for an Education Health and Care Plan (EHCP)

If a mainstream school is unable to or refuses to meet your child's needs you may choose to get an EHCP (or IEP if you are in the US). This is a lengthy document that outlines all of the education, health and social care needs your child has, and how they must be supported at school. The EHCP covers your child until they are 25, so you can apply for one any time. Although they support up to age 25, they do not cover help at university. However, they do deal with apprenticeships and college.

The first thing to do is to ask the school to apply for what is called an EHCNA, which is an Education Health and Care Needs Assessment. The school SENCo is usually the person you need to approach about this. If the school is unsupportive, you can apply yourself. Your local authority's website will have more information on how to do this. If the school says something like, 'you will never get an EHCP for your child', ignore them and carry on with applying yourself.

It is very common to be refused an EHCNA the first time around. When the local authority refuses your application, they will provide information on how you can appeal, so do that. Carry on until the council agrees to carry out the EHCNA.

Your child's needs will be assessed by education, health and care professionals, including an educational psychologist. If you are concerned that your child has learning difficulties, insist that the educational psychologist carries out a full cognitive assessment at this point. The professional reports will be fed back to the council for them to determine if your child should have an EHCP. If they decline to give your child an EHCP, appeal their decision.

Once they agree to the EHCP, you and the school will work out the details of the plan. An EHCP is a complex document which requires very specific language. It can feel very daunting. The process of getting an EHCP is meant to take 20 weeks but generally takes much longer, sometimes over a year. There is a wealth of information about the EHCP process and who can help you with it to be found at wdisbook.com/resources.

THE LAW IS ON YOUR SIDE

A great way to boost your confidence and assertiveness is to understand the laws that protect your child's right to an education and all that entails. In the UK, these are:

- The SEND Code of Practice

- The Equality Act 2010

- The Children and Families Act 2014.

These crucial pieces of legislation outline the statutory responsibilities of education settings and provide guidance regarding non-statutory issues. They are available online and are written in clear language. If you are having a tough time with your child's school, it may even be worth having a hard copy of each printed for easier reference.

Knowing what the school's legal obligations are is extremely useful because then it's not just you nagging them but the government. Quoting passages from the Equality Act or SEND Code of Practice may not make you very popular with the school. However, it will make it clear to them that you know what you are talking about and that not providing appropriate support for your child is actually illegal.

Be prepared

Before you begin the EHCP process, you will want to be sure you are organized. I have mentioned this before but it bears repeating: keep every scrap of paper and every email to do with your child and school (and their health, as well) in some way that works for you. I've known parents who have beautiful lever arch files with all of their child's documents and then there are people like me who just have everything in one box. You will need these things for the EHCP. Reports from speech and language therapists, occupational therapists, educational psychologists, diagnosis letters and anything else to do with your child is all useful for the EHCP process.

Get in writing everything that the school is currently doing for your child. They may tell you that they are not doing anything because they feel your child does not require any support at school. However, if you press them you may find that there are all sorts of things in place that you had no idea of. It may be that your child is allowed to leave the classroom when they are feeling anxious, or that they are allowed to sit in a quiet room, or that they are allowed to eat lunch at a different time to the other children. Finding out what is already in place for your child is a strong first step to getting them better support.

Keep a diary of all the things that aren't as they should be. For example, they won't keep your child in school full time, they won't let your son or daughter have movement breaks during the day, or they won't take your child on school trips. All of these things are good evidence.

Read through the SEND Code of Practice; you can easily find this online. You may be able to find ways the school is not supporting your child. For example, if the school will not allow your child to go on field trips because they feel that they cannot support them, but they also will not allow you to accompany your child on these trips, that is discrimination. Similarly, look at your local authority's SEN protocol to see if it highlights any ways the school is not supporting your child.

The nitty gritty

Ensure that the EHCP contains no 'woolly language'. It must give 'SMART' goals – goals that are Specific, Measurable, Achievable, Relevant and Time-based. For example, it cannot say that your child should have 'regular speech and language sessions' as this is too vague. The frequency of the sessions must be clearly spelled out, for example 'one session per week for an hour each session'.

Get help and stay calm

The upside of the SEND system being so messed up is that there is a lot of help to be had for you in dealing with this process. There are many charities and websites that will guide you through the process. See wdisbook.com/resources for details of these. Every local authority has what is called a SENDIAS – a Special Educational Needs and Disabilities Information and Advice Service. Search the internet for 'SENDIAS + your area' (for example, 'SENDIAS Harrogate') to find your local one. You may need to get legal advice to get help with your child's EHCP. You may also need to hire a private educational psychologist to assess your child to give a clear picture of what they need at school. You may be able to get legal aid or other financial help. It is possible to get what you need without hiring professionals (I did) but it takes more time and effort on your part.

Above all, keep calm. Treat getting an EHCP like a business project. Work out your steps and put one foot in front of the other until you get the job done. Remember – you will get there, and once you have it, you are done. It will feel like it's going on forever, but it really will end and your child will be better supported.

THE THING ABOUT TEACHERS AND SENCOS

When your child first goes to school, you will earnestly believe that all of the teaching staff that they encounter will have a lot of autism training and know exactly how to support them. Sadly, this is far from the reality. Most teachers have had an afternoon of 'Autism 101'-style training, and this may have been many years ago. They may have had an autistic pupil in their class in the past and think what worked for that child will work for yours.

You will very quickly come to understand that many teachers know very little about autism. Teachers are not to blame for this. We live in a society that vastly undervalues teachers and invests very little in SEND (Special Educational Needs and Disabilities) support.

Similarly, the school SENCo (Special Educational Needs Co-ordinator) may not have much autism training or experience. He or she may not have chosen to become a SENCo; they may have been pushed into the role by senior staff at the school. In addition to being a SENCo they may also be a teacher. Therefore, they may only have one afternoon a week to manage the needs of 30 or more children with SEN. Or they may be the SENCo for more than one school.

Unfortunately, it is often down to us as parents to educate the educators. If you find yourself in this situation, please do this with grace and patience. These are often hard-working individuals who want to do well but may not have been given the training or resources to do this efficiently.

Moving from mainstream to specialist provision or Education Other Than at School (EOTAS)

There may come a time when you must decide that mainstream school is not the best place for your child. This can be a painful decision. My daughter has always been in specialist provision. When I chose this for her, I felt it was absolutely the right thing to do, and it was. However, I still remember the first day of school, taking her into a classroom that was *very* different to the one I had envisioned for my child. That experience broke me a bit, so I truly understand how this decision can be hard.

The way to choose a specialist school is to have a look around at what schools are available in your local area. There are many autism-specific special schools, and there are also pan-disability schools that cover a wide range of needs. You must go and visit the schools. Your parental gut will tell you immediately which schools are right and which ones will not do.

You will need to have an EHCP for your child in order for them to go to a special school. If it is an autism-specific school, you will likely need a diagnosis for your child to attend. Each school should have their eligibility requirements on their website.

When choosing a school, don't just think about academic issues but also if your child's social and emotional needs will be catered for and their talents and skills nurtured. For example, if your child is very musical or artistic, check to be sure the school offers options to support these talents.

I believe that specialist schools are the right place for many of our children. They can provide so much more specialist care than a mainstream school. Speech and language, social skills and occupational therapies are often provided at special schools. Unique experiences such as visiting local businesses and taking interesting day trips are also common. Some schools have vocational training opportunities. My daughter's school has a huge horticultural department so that the children can learn to grow flowers and do landscaping.

Education Other Than at School (EOTAS) may be an option if your child simply cannot attend school for a wide variety of factors.

Anxiety can be a huge issue when it comes to school, and so a different type of provision may be required. My daughter has been out of full-time education for years and now has a mix of specialist provision and EOTAS. Your child's school should know what EOTAS options are available and how your child can access them. Generally speaking, a child will need an EHCP to access EOTAS. However, this can vary depending on the local authority and the child's situation.

It is a tough decision but as I've said a fair few times now: trust your gut. If you feel that mainstream education is simply not working for your child, a special school or EOTAS is likely the answer. Remember also that if your child is struggling to fit in at a mainstream school, being in a special school surrounded by other children like them and people who understand their needs could result in a huge reduction in stress and anxiety.

CHAPTER 18

How to Engage with Your Child (When They Don't Want to Engage with You)

You may be given well-intentioned advice, as I was, that you need to bring your child into your world. By nature, autistic individuals are self-involved; the word 'autism' comes from the Greek 'autós' which means 'self'. To bring an autistic individual into your world, you must first join them in theirs.

I talk in other parts of this book about how, at the beginning of my autism journey, I spent a lot of time on the internet, reading blog posts, buying books and so called 'autism supplements' and other things. I was so scared of what autism would mean for my daughter's future that I did this instead of spending time with her. I didn't know how to help her and I felt I was failing her. What I wasn't doing was what was most needed. I wasn't spending time with and connecting with my child. It's painful to share this with you now, but it is vital information for you to have so that you don't make the same mistake.

During the period when I was distracting myself from spending time with my daughter, another issue made our interaction difficult. From the ages of about two to four years old, my daughter didn't want to play with me. I'd give her a toy and she didn't know what to do with it. I'd try to engage her with a game, but she had no interest. This was confusing and upsetting. How could I get her to play and play with me?

Eventually, I realized I was going about this in the wrong way.

Instead of getting her to play with me, I needed to play with her. I started by getting physically on her level. If she was on the floor, I'd get down on the floor. If she was sitting at the table, I'd sit with her. I followed her around, and instead of pushing different toys at her, I'd play with whatever she was playing with, commenting on each thing, 'now we are playing with the blocks. The tower is falling over! Boom!' I followed her lead, literally shadowing her around the house and keeping a running commentary of everything we did.

It's important to note that during this time, she took very little notice of me. This was difficult as it felt like a rejection. However, I persevered and I'm glad I did. This practice of being on her level and commenting on everything we did became a deeply ingrained habit that I still have now. Although it didn't feel like it at the time, my efforts were slowly but surely paying off and creating a bond between us.

My daughter was nonspeaking until the age of four-and-a-half, but I copied the sounds she made. This delighted her. I found that mimicking her movements had a similar effect. I learned to do this by studying something called Intensive Interaction. During this time, I made another crucial discovery: my daughter did not know how to play with toys, and it was down to me to teach her.

I soon realized that she was not interested in the toys other children her age played with. She loved (and still loves) cause-and-effect toys, ones that light up and make sounds. She was not interested in dolls, cuddly toys, games, and most other toys children her age enjoyed. I began to pay close attention to the things she enjoyed and the things she didn't. I stopped looking at the specified age range for any given toy and just bought what I knew she would like.

A huge breakthrough came when we started making music together. Musical play is a wonderful way to engage with your child. Music has no rules. You don't have to have a goal with music, or even a start and finish. My daughter loves making music. We first bought her a toy electric keyboard. She quickly learned how to play the theme songs to her favourite TV programmes. She soon graduated to a full-sized electric keyboard. She would play and I would sing, or beat a drum or xylophone.

Music encouraged her to make sounds which eventually became words. She had music therapy which encouraged turn-taking and social and communication skills development.

Joining your child in their world has no age limit. Whatever age your child is, get involved with what they do. Even if you have no interest in their favourite band, video game, preteen book series or other obsession, learn about it anyway. This is how to connect with your child. If they can have conversations with you about whatever it is they most love, your bond will be strengthened. You may even find you enjoy learning about your child's special interest!

Here are some examples of how I have engaged with my daughter in this way:

- She loves to draw and make recordings of her drawings. I spend several hours a week playing cameraman for her.

- My daughter is very musical and has taught herself to play the piano. I have zero musical talent but am taking guitar lessons so that I can play with her as I know this will be fun.

- I've set up an online shop to sell items featuring the characters she draws. She loves coming up with new designs and I love managing the techy side of this venture.

Autism affects everyone differently. Only by spending time with your child will you understand their unique brand of autism. You will build a solid bond that will make it easier to weather difficult times down the line.

WHAT ABOUT ABA?

Applied Behavioural Analysis (ABA) is another one of those things that often appears when you are first searching the internet for ways to help your child. It is very controversial and rightfully so. However, it is not a black and white issue; it has a few grey areas.

ABA was developed in the 1960s by a psychologist called Ivar Ole Lovaas as a way to help autistic children appear more 'normal'. We have to remember that at this time, it was commonplace and acceptable to institutionalize autistic children. Lovaas's ABA was seen as a way of helping families avoid this fate for their children. In this it was successful.

The general aim of ABA is to make a person appear less autistic. It is widely used with autistic children. The methods can be invasive and cruel. There is a great deal of information on the internet about autistic adults who were severely traumatized by the ABA therapy they were subjected to as children.

The grey area with ABA is that it is not all about making autistic children appear less autistic. Some ABA therapy is designed simply to help autistic children engage with life in a more fulfilling way. Attention Autism, PECS and TEACCH® are all thought to be ABA therapies.

Choosing an ABA-based therapy for your son or daughter is an extremely personal choice. If you are considering going down.

this route, please spend time researching the therapist to ensure that you have a very solid understanding of their aims with your child. A therapy that helps a child communicate more effectively is perfectly appropriate. A treatment aimed at lessening or removing your child's autistic traits must be avoided at all costs.

CHAPTER 19

Be Here Now

Every parent worries about their child's future. Will she be happy? Will he be healthy? For parents of autistic children, this worry can become overwhelming if it's not kept in check. Will he live independently? Will she ever have a job or a relationship? We also worry about what will happen when we are no longer here. Our worries are enormous and will be all-consuming if we allow them to be.

It's natural to worry about your child. However, if you spend all your time worrying about the future, you will miss the amazing things that are happening today. You will rob yourself of the joy of your child's smile, the sound of their laugh or the funny thing they said in the car.

We are only in control of ourselves, our thoughts and our actions. We are not in control of people at school, our partner, family members or our children. We are not in control of the future. There is no way to predict how your child will develop over time, or where they will be in five, ten or 15 years' time.

Think of how much the world has changed over the past 11 years or even five years. The internet creates endless opportunities for people to make a living online. Before the Covid-19 pandemic, many employers believed it was impossible for their staff to work productively from home. How times have changed!

My point is that wherever your child ends up in life, there will be opportunities for them to make a living. It may not be in a Monday to Friday, 9–5, working-in-an-office type job, but fewer and fewer people are working this way these days.

Suzanne is an accountant. Her teenage autistic son is also keen on numbers and so she is very gently teaching him how to be an accountant. Her goal is that, if he would like to do so when the time comes, she and her son will work together in an accountancy business. Similarly, Paul organized for himself and his step-son to train as electricians so that they could have a business together.

I often tell the story of Brad Fremmerlid, an autistic man living in Canada. Brad's dad wanted to help his son find a way to make a living. He realized that Brad has a real skill for putting together flat-pack furniture, and so he created Made by Brad, a business that enables Brad to work. Brad is nonspeaking and cannot read, but he is making a living.

My daughter is a prolific artist. She draws funny little characters all day. I recently set up a shop to sell her drawings, with the profit going into her trust fund. Although she is only 13, I feel this is an important step to take now to get her drawings seen by the public. Who knows where it will go?

As I've mentioned, I'm autistic and have ADHD. I've managed to carve out an interesting work life for myself. I am self-employed and work from home which gives me time and space to work however I need to on any given day.

Don't underestimate your child. He or she may not take a conventional route into employment but with flexibility and an open mind, you can help them to find meaningful work.

Do not allow yourself to be consumed by worrying about your child's future. You will paralyse yourself with fear, and this is unproductive. Not only will this adversely affect your mental health, but it will make it impossible for you to do what you can to support your child today. You will overwhelm yourself with the belief that you must solve all of your child's problems right now, which will make it impossible for you to do anything.

Similarly, do not spend your time regretting things in the past. Many parents do this, beating themselves up for not knowing sooner that their child was autistic. They may also regret not working on this thing or that thing to help their child when the child was younger. Worrying in this way is of no benefit to anyone. You can only do your best with the resources you have at any given time. Be kind to yourself.

Just be here now, in this moment, with your wonderful child.

Where Do I Start?

A poem for parents and carers who are new to autism

BY KATE LAINE-TONER

First things first: take a deep breath;
everything is going to be alright.
You will get through this.

Be gentle with yourself; you are doing the best that you can.
Keep hold of your own interests, dreams and desires.
Look after yourself first; you cannot pour from an empty cup.

As far as possible, be on good terms with the people around you.
Avoid those who are judgmental and ignorant; they are poison to the spirit.

Remain strong in the face of adversity, the noise and drama;
you can survive anything life throws at you!
Take time to recover when life is hard, but never give up.

Speak your truth calmly and clearly.
Trust your gut instinct; it is always right.
Listen to others, even to those who seem very different from you;
They, too, have their story and may touch your heart.

Remember that comparison is the thief of joy.
Do not compare your child or your family with others;
only you know what is best for yourself.
Celebrate successes no matter how small they may seem.

Be yourself; you are a gift to the universe.
Do not hoard your knowledge; share it freely and
listen with care to the stories of others in your shoes.

If friends abandon you, make new ones that understand.
Hold them close, for there is safety in numbers
and great comfort to be found in shared experiences.

Carry those who are weak as others will do the same for you.
Ask not what others can do for you, but what you can do for them;
joy comes from helping those in need.

Do not distress yourself with unfounded worries.
Arm yourself with the light of knowledge; fear blooms in the dark.
Do not suffer in silence; share your troubles:
'a problem shared is a problem halved'.

Despite disappointments and broken dreams,
the world is full of beauty and wonder.
There is still happiness to be found –
in laughter, friendship and simple pleasures.